YORK NOTES

DU   ND
AR   AGE
& PR   POETRY

N   NNINGTON

Longman

York Press

The right of David Pinnington to be id̲
has been asserted by him in accordanc̲
Copyright, Designs and Patents Act 198̲

YORK PRESS
322 Old Brompton Road, London SW5

PEARSON EDUCATION LIMITED
Edinburgh Gate, Harlow,
Essex CM20 2JE, United Kingdom
Associated companies, branches and representatives throughout the world

First published 2003
Eighth impression 2008

ISBN: 978-0-582-77263-2

Designed by Michelle Cannatella
Illustrated by Judy Stevens
Typeset by Land & Unwin (Data Sciences), Bugbrooke, Northamptonshire
Produced by Pearson Education Asia Limited, Hong Kong

CONTENTS

York Notes are designed to give you a broader perspective on works of literature studied at GCSE and equivalent levels. With examination requirements changing in the twenty-first century, we have made a number of significant changes to this new series. We continue to help students to reach their own interpretations of the text but York Notes now have important extra-value new features.

You will discover that York Notes are genuinely interactive. The new **Checkpoint** features make sure that you can test your knowledge and broaden your understanding. You will also be directed to excellent websites, books and films where you can follow up ideas for yourself.

The **Resources** section has been updated and an entirely new section has been devoted to how to improve your grade. Careful reading and application of the principles laid out in the Resources section guarantee improved performance.

The **Detailed summaries** include an easy-to-follow skeleton structure of the poems, while the section on **Language and style** has been extended to offer an in-depth discussion of the poets' techniques.

The Contents page shows the structure of this study guide. However, there is no need to read from the beginning to the end as you would with a novel, play or poem. Use the Notes in the way that suits you. Our aim is to help you with your understanding of the poems, not to dictate how you should learn.

Our authors are practising English teachers and examiners who have used their experience to offer a whole range of **Examiner's secrets** – useful hints to encourage exam success.

The General Editor of this series is John Polley, Senior GCSE Examiner and former Head of English at Harrow Way Community School, Andover.

The author of these Notes, David Pinnington, has been an English examiner for A level and GCSE. He has written York Notes for *Twelfth Night*, *The Tempest* and *Henry IV Part One*.

The text used in these Notes is the AQA Anthology for GCSE English/English Literature (Specification A for 2004).

HOW TO STUDY A POEM

A poem differs from a piece of prose writing because it is freer in its structure, and it often contains a deliberate **rhyme** and/or **rhythm**. When reading a poem, each of these aspects should be considered:

STRUCTURE: The poet has made conscious choices to organise the poem as it appears on the page. Try to understand the poet's thinking behind:

- The organisation of the lines (e.g. into verses)

- Any repetition of lines or varying lengths of line

- Whether lines are **end-stopped** or whether the sense carries over to the next line

RHYME: Consider the rhyming scheme and ask yourself these questions:

- What, if any, is the rhyming scheme?

- Are the rhymes exact or approximate and for what purpose?

- Do some lines have rhyming words within them and why?

- If there are no rhymes, why does the line end where it does?

RHYTHM: Turn to the rhythm of the poem and listen for:

- Which words are stressed

- Whether there is a pattern of sound which creates a mood

- Whether this mood suits the subject matter

SUBJECT MATTER AND THEME: Just like a novel or a play, a poem has a subject matter and a theme. Once you have identified these, consider why the poet has drawn on that particular subject matter to illustrate an idea or develop the theme.

 DID YOU KNOW?

The word 'poetry' comes from the Greek word *poesis*, meaning 'making' or 'creating'. People have been writing poetry for thousands of years – the earliest we have dates back to about 3000 BC.

DUFFY/ARMITAGE – LIFE AND WORKS

CONTEXT

1954 May 6: First anti-nuclear protest march to Aldermaston. Dylan Thomas: *Under Milk Wood*; Golding: *Lord of the Flies*; British Top 20 begins: first No.1 was *Hold My Hand* by Don Cornel

1955 on Carol Ann Duffy born Glasgow, Scotland. Education: Stafford High School, Liverpool University (Philosophy)

1955 TV starts in Britain. Britain explodes her first hydrogen bomb

1957 First comprehensive school opens in London. Angry Young Men movement in English literature. Notting Hill Race riots. Munich air disaster – Manchester United team members killed. Beckett: *Krapp's Last Tape*

1962 Helen Shapiro: *Walking Back to Happiness*. First live TV between US and Europe (Telstar). Oct 24: Cuba missile crisis – brink of nuclear war

1963 on Simon Armitage born Huddersfield, England. Education: Portsmouth Polytechnic (Geography); Manchester University (Psychology)

1963 Nov 22: President Kennedy assassinated in Dallas. Pop music: Beatles achieve international fame — release of *Please Please Me*, *From Me to You*, *She Loves You*, *I Want to Hold Your Hand*

1973 Duffy: *Fleshweathercock*, a pamphlet of poems, published by Outposts Press

1973 Jan 1: Britain enters Common Market. Jan 27: Vietnam ceasefire agreement signed. Dec 31: Miners strike and oil crisis precipitate 'three-day week' to conserve power

1982 Duffy: *Fifth Last Song*.

1985 Duffy: *Standing Female Nude*

1987 Duffy: *Selling Manhattan*

1981 Jul 29: Wedding of Prince Charles and Lady Diana Spencer. Riots in Brixton, South London – and 30 other British cities

1988 Dec 21: Lockerbie disaster – Pan Am flight 103 explodes over Scotland

DUFFY/ARMITAGE – LIFE AND WORKS

1989 Armitage: *Zoom*. First book-length collection. Poetry Book Society Choice, short-listed for the Whitworth Prize. Duffy: *I Wouldn't Thank You for a Valentine*

1992 Duffy: Co-editor of *I Wouldn't Thank You for a Valentine*: *Poems for Young Feminists* with Trisha Rafferty. Armitage: *Kid*. Won the '*Sunday Times* Young Writer of the Year'

1993 Duffy: *Mean Time*. Armitage: *Book of Matches*

1994 Duffy: *Selected Poems*

1995 Armitage: *Dead Sea Poems*. The collection finishes with the long poem 'Five Eleven Ninety Nine', about the last Bonfire Night of the Millennium

1996 Duffy: *Stopping for Death*: *Poems of Death and Loss*

1997 Duffy: *Selling Manhattan*

1998 Armitage: *All Points North*

1999 Armitage: *Killing Time*. Duffy: *The World's Wife*

2000 Armitage: *Selected Poems*

2001 Duffy: Awarded CBE

2002 Armitage: *The Universal Home Doctor* and *Travelling Songs*. Duffy: *Feminine Gospels*

CONTEXT

1989 Poll Tax implemented in Scotland. House of Commons proceedings first televised. Berlin Wall torn down

1990 Margaret Thatcher resigns as Conservative party leader (and Prime Minister). Poll Tax implemented in England and Wales – riots. Aug 2: Iraq invades Kuwait

1993 July: The European Union (EU) established. Betty Boothroyd becomes first woman Speaker of the House of Commons (to 2000). Elizabeth II becomes first British Monarch to pay Income Tax

1997 May: Labour landslide victory in Britain. August: Princess of Wales killed in car crash

1998 Good Friday peace agreement in Northern Ireland

1999 Nov 11: Hereditary Peers no longer have right to sit in House of Lords. World population reaches 6 billion (estimate)

2001 September 11: Massive terrorist attack on the United States

2002 Twelve major countries in Europe start using the euro instead of their national currencies; the UK stays out

PRE-1914 POETS – LIFE AND WORKS

1564 William Shakespeare born

1572 Ben Jonson born

1586 Execution of Charles Tichborne. *Tichborne's Elegy* published

1609 Shakespeare's *Sonnets* published

1616 Death of William Shakespeare. *On my first Sonne*, Ben Jonson

1637 Death of Ben Jonson

1730 Oliver Goldsmith born

1757 William Blake born

1770 Wordsworth born. *The Village Schoolmaster*, Oliver Goldsmith

1774 Death of Oliver Goldsmith

1789 *The Little Boy Lost*, William Blake. *The Little Boy Found*, William Blake

1793 John Clare born

1807 *The Affliction of Margaret*, William Wordsworth

1809 Alfred Tennyson born

1812 Robert Browning born

1819 Walt Whitman born

1827 Death of William Blake

1840 Thomas Hardy born

1841 *Sonnet*, John Clare

1842 *Ulysses*, Alfred Tennyson

CONTEXT

1558 Accession of Queen Elizabeth I

1564 Death of Michelangelo

1586 Treaty of Berwick establishes a defensive alliance between England and Scotland.

1587 Execution of Mary, Queen of Scots

1588 Defeat of the Spanish Armada

1603 Death of Queen Elizabeth I

1608 Galileo first uses the telescope

1769 Birth of Napoleon

1770 Steam engine patented; James Cook discovers New South Wales

1776 Declaration of American Independence

1789 French Revolution

1793 First free English settlers in Australia

1807 Britain abolishes slave trade

1809 Charles Darwin born

1812 First tin cans produced in England for preserving food

1815 Battle of Waterloo

1819 Peterloo Massacre

1827 First successful photograph taken

1837 Accession of Queen Victoria

1840 Penny postage stamp introduced

1842 British massacred in Khyber Pass

PRE-1914 POETS – LIFE AND WORKS	CONTEXT
1844 Gerard Manley Hopkins born	**1844** First Factory Act
1845 *My Last Duchess*, Robert Browning *The Laboratory*, Robert Browning	**1845** Irish Potato Famine
	1848 General revolutionary movement throughout Europe
1850 Death of Wordsworth. Tennyson becomes Poet Laureate	**1850** Creation of jeans by Oscar Levi Strauss for Californian gold prospectors
1851 *The Eagle*, Alfred Tennyson	**1851** The Great Exhibition in London
1856 *Patrolling Barnegat*, Walt Whitman	**1856** End of the Crimean War
	1859 Darwin's *On the Origin of Species*
1864 Death of John Clare	**1861** Outbreak of American Civil War
1865 William B. Yeats born	**1865** End of American Civil War
1881 *Inversnaid*, Gerard Manley Hopkins	**1881** Birth of Pablo Picasso
1884 Tennyson becomes a Baron	**1888** The 'Jack the Ripper' murders
1889 Death of Robert Browning. Death of Gerard Manley Hopkins	**1889** Birth of Adolf Hitler
1892 Death of Alfred, Lord Tennyson. Death of Walt Whitman	
1899 *The Song of the Old Mother*, W. B. Yeats	**1899** Outbreak of Boer War
	1901 Death of Queen Victoria
1902 *The Man He Killed*, Thomas Hardy	**1902** End of Boer War
	1912 Sinking of *Titanic*
	1914 Outbreak of First World War
1918 Hopkins' poetry published	**1918** End of First World War
	1926 Birth of Queen Elizabeth II
1928 Death of Thomas Hardy	**1928** Discovery of penicillin
	1937 Accession of George VI
1939 Death of William B. Yeats	**1939** Outbreak of Second World War

SETTING AND BACKGROUND

CAROL ANN DUFFY

Carol Ann Duffy was born 23 December 1955, in Glasgow, Scotland. At the age of five, her family moved to Stafford when her father got a job with English Electric (GEC). There she went to St Joseph's convent school and was encouraged to write poetry by her teacher. Later she attended Stafford High School for Girls. When she was sixteen Carol Ann Duffy met the Liverpool poet Adrian Henri.

She was eighteen when she published her first pamphlet of poems, *Fleshweathercock*, in 1973. In 1974, she went to Liverpool University and three years later graduated with an honours degree in Philosophy. Her reading in philosophy brought her into contact with the writings of Ludwig Wittgenstein whose ideas about the limitations of language, as a means of communication, became a theme in several of her poems.

DID YOU KNOW?

In the 1980s Carol Ann Duffy wrote several plays, including *Take My Husband*, 1982, *Cavern of Dreams*, 1984, *Little Women, Big Boys*, 1986, and *Loss*, 1986, a play for radio broadcast by the BBC.

After graduating she worked for Granada Television and then moved to London where she lived until 1995. A C. Day Lewis Fellowship enabled her to work as a writer in residence in East End schools between 1982 and 1984.

Carol Ann Duffy has won many prizes and awards for her writing. In 1983 she won first prize in the National Poetry Competition, and she received a Scottish Arts Council Award for *Standing Female Nude*. She received the Eric Gregory Award in 1984. Other awards include the Somerset Maugham Award (1987), the Dylan Thomas Award (1989), the Cholmondeley Award (1992), the Whitbread Award, the Forward Poetry Prize, a Scottish Arts Council Book Award (1993), the Lannan Award (USA) in 1995 and the Signal Poetry Award (1997). In 1995, she was awarded the OBE. She was made a Fellow of the Royal Society of Letters in 1999 and awarded a CBE for services to literature in 2001.

The Poems

Carol Ann Duffy seems to have a great interest in **dramatic monologues** and seven of the eight poems you will be studying are all written in the 'voice' of a particular character. In her book of poems, *The World's Wife* (1999), all the poems are in the female voices of characters drawn from myth and history, such as 'Queen Herod' and 'Mrs Darwin'. These are women usually excluded from the history books, or women like 'Delilah' or 'Eurydice' whose identities have been defined by men. In some of the poems, Duffy has reversed the roles and the sex to tell a familiar story from a female perspective – 'Queen Kong', the 'Kray Sisters'.

'Elvis's Twin Sister', **'Anne Hathaway'** and **'Salome'** are from this collection. They are all women connected to famous men who have been given a 'voice' by Carol Ann Duffy. An earlier example of the female monologue is also included, **'Havisham'**, which vocalises the bitterness of Miss Havisham, the time-trapped jilted bride from Charles Dickens's *Great Expectations.*

Two other dramatic monologues are **'Education for Leisure'** and **'Stealing'**. These reveal another aspect of Duffy's interest in this form: the way it allows the writer to get into the mind of characters that are very different to herself, such as thieves, rapists or psychopaths. Duffy has written several poems using the male voice of this type of character and they have become very popular with her readers.

'Before You Were Mine' reflects another aspect of Carol Ann Duffy's work, namely her ability to write about her own personal experience and the people she has known and loved. **'Before You Were Mine'** is based on her mother's life in Scotland before Carol Ann was born. The poet imagines her mother as a happy-go-lucky girl, not unlike her namesake, Marilyn Monroe.

'We Remember Your Childhood Well' is a kind of monologue except that the speaker is a choral 'we', the collective voice of parental adults who are redefining the childhood of a child. A nameless trauma has occurred that they clearly do not want to face up to.

When she was interviewed after the publication of *The World's Wife* in 1999, Carol Ann Duffy said, 'Each poem had to be personally

EXAMINER'S SECRET

Feel free to interpret poetry in any way you want! After all, it's not – yet – against the law to be original. As long as you are able to make a convincing argument in support of your interpretations, just about anything goes.

honest, and have some kind of autobiographical element in it, whether it had happened to me or whether it was an emotional or intellectual truth' (*Guardian*, Saturday, September 25, 1999). This perhaps is one of the reasons why she has such a wide readership and has become in the words of one critic, 'the representative poet of her day'

SIMON ARMITAGE

DID YOU KNOW?

Simon Armitage uses a character invented by the American poet, Weldon Kees, in several of his poems. The character's name is 'Robinson'.

Simon Armitage was born in 1963 and lives in West Yorkshire. One of his earliest childhood memories of a literary experience is 'reading *The Wind in the Willows* sat in the airing cupboard, where it was warm and very comfortable on top of the clean towels'. He was not particularly interested in poetry as a child and a lot of his reading was confined to 'catalogues, instruction manuals and lists'. At school he describes himself as 'a very poor student up until the final push in the Upper Sixth'. However, at his comprehensive school he did encounter the writing of Hughes, Larkin and Shakespeare, which he enjoyed reading in spite of his prejudices!

Simon Armitage began writing poems when he was a student at Portsmouth studying for a degree in Geography. He has described these early efforts as 'uninformed teenage nonsense. I still have it hidden away under the bed, and look at it if I ever feel like melting away with embarrassment'. However, it was when he returned to the North to take an MA in Social Work at Manchester University that he began to write in earnest. He joined a writing workshop run by Peter Sansom, who became something of a mentor for Simon Armitage: 'the composite critic/audience sitting on my shoulder, watching the words as they land on the page, falling backwards off his chair or curling his nose up!'. At this time he was very influenced by American poetry.

After working as a probation officer for six years, Simon Armitage became a freelance writer and broadcaster. To date he has published nine volumes of poetry including *Killing Time* (Faber & Faber, 1999) and *Selected Poems* (Faber & Faber, 2000). In addition to writing for radio, television and film, he is the author of four stage plays, including *Mister Heracles*, and, in 2001 Penguin published his first novel, *Little Green Man*.

Simon Armitage has taught at the University of Leeds and the University of Iowa's Writers' Workshop, and currently teaches at Manchester Metropolitan University. With Robert Crawford he has edited *The Penguin Anthology of Poetry from Britain and Ireland Since 1945*, and two further collections of poetry, *The Universal Home Doctor* and *Travelling Songs* (Faber & Faber, 2002).

The Poems

Simon Armitage has said, 'A lot of my poems are about feelings, so one way of approaching a poem is to read it, see how it makes you feel and then say why. One thing you shouldn't do is assume there's some kind of key that will "turn" this poem, or that there's some code that you've got to press' (quoted in *Working with the English Anthology*, Heinemann, 1998). Several of the poems you are studying deal with powerful basic emotions that are easy to identify with, such as attachment to parents, growing up and reflecting on the way your attitudes differ from theirs, dealing with other people in the world, and contemplating what it means to grow old and die. This should be a starting point for appreciating and enjoying Simon Armitage's poetry: he writes about everyday things in ordinary language.

The poem **'Kid'** is the title poem from Simon Armitage's third book of poems (1999). It is fairly representative of the themes of that collection, which includes poems describing domestic tensions, the chaos and anarchy which seem to exist not far beneath the surface of people's lives.

Five of the poems – **'Mother, any distance'**, **'My father thought it bloody queer'**, **'Those bastards in their mansions'**, **'I've made out a will'**, and **'Hitcher'** – are taken from *Book of Matches* (1993), a collection of more personal poems containing three sequences: *Book of Matches* which is a **sonnet** sequence of psychological self-portraits told during the length of time it takes a match to burn; *Becoming of Age* (of which **'Hitcher'** is one) and *Reading the Bans*, a series of poems about Simon Armitage's marriage.

'November' is from *Zoom!* – Simon Armitage's first book-length collection, published by Bloodaxe in 1989. This collection contains

 DID YOU KNOW?
Simon Armitage is the only poet on the English Literature curriculum with a degree in Geography!

EXAMINER'S SECRET

The examiners are more interested in what you have to say about the poem than what you know about the poet.

some of the most characteristic of his poems and it is one in which many believe he first expressed the unique Armitage voice. As Peter Sansom says: 'He has found his voice early, and it really is his *own* voice – his language and rhythms draw from the Pennine village where he lives: robust, no-nonsense and (above all) honest'.

'Homecoming' is a poem that explores the uncertainties of memory and how the past and the present are conveyed in poetry. Although Simon Armitage has written many poems that appear to be autobiographical, they never represent a straightforward connection between experience and poetry. 'Homecoming' is typical of the ambiguity that is present in all his best work. 'Hitcher', however, is a more dramatic first-person narrative, a character **monologue** recounting an act of casual violence that draws comparison with some of Carol Ann Duffy's poems.

Pre- 1914 Poetry Bank

BLAKE, WILLIAM: *The Little Boy Lost/Found*

William Blake was born in 1757 to a very poor London hosier. Apart from a brief spell in Sussex, Blake lived in or near to London all his life. He received little formal schooling, yet his work bears witness to an extremely wide range of reading: the Bible, Milton, Greek and Latin classic literature. His spiritual and intellectual development was greatly influenced by his brother, Robert, who died at the age of twenty. All of Blake's work contains an extraordinary mix of apocalyptic vision, political fervour, reworkings of Christian myth and psychological exploration. Like Wordsworth, Blake was politically both a radical and a libertarian. He was committed to the principles of social, political and sexual equality. Blake died in 1827 and was buried in a pauper's grave.

BROWNING, ROBERT: *My Last Duchess/ The Laboratory*

Robert Browning was born in 1812 in the London suburb of Camberwell. He was the son of a clerk at the Bank of England and

CHECK THE FILM

The classic film, *The Barretts of Wimpole Street* is based upon the relationship of Robert Browning and Elizabeth Barrett

was extremely intelligent. In 1846, he married the poet Elizabeth Barrett in dramatic circumstances and they eloped to Italy where they lived until her death in 1861. Robert Browning returned to London with their son. Robert soon achieved greater recognition and, along with Alfred Tennyson, was regarded as the leading poet of the Victorian age. He died in 1889.

CLARE, JOHN: *Sonnet*

John Clare was born in 1793, the son of a farm labourer in Northamptonshire in the English Midlands. He received only a basic education and left school at the age of twelve to become a ploughboy. He also worked in a public house and as a gardener. His first collection of poems was published in 1820. It sold well and he became known as the 'Ploughman Poet' who wrote in a simple accessible way about the simple pleasures of the countryside. His subsequent publications were less popular and he fell victim to mental instability. He died in 1864.

DID YOU KNOW?
John Clare escaped from an asylum in Epping Forest in 1841 and walked 80 miles to his home surviving by 'eating the grass by the side of the road'

GOLDSMITH, OLIVER: *The Village Schoolmaster*

Oliver Goldsmith was born into an Irish rural family, his father was a clergyman. When he went to Trinity College in Dublin he was so poor that he had to act as a servant to the more fortunate students. He started writing to try and pay his bills though he was still deeply in debt when he died in 1774. He tried his hand at every type of writing including journalism and he was admired by his contemporaries for the clarity and elegance of his expression.

DID YOU KNOW?
As well as being a writer, Goldsmith was also an able flautist.

HARDY, THOMAS: *The Man He Killed*

Hardy was born on 2 June 1840 in Higher Bockhampton in Dorset, near Dorchester. His father was a master mason and building contractor. Hardy's mother, whose tastes were literary, provided for his education and the young boy studied Latin, French and began reading widely. Between 1871 and 1897 Hardy wrote many novels set in the West Country in the early part of the nineteenth century, *Far from the Madding Crowd* (1874) and *Tess of the d'Urbervilles* (1891) being among the most celebrated. But Hardy preferred to write poetry and regarded his novels as a source of income.

JONSON, BEN: *On my first Sonne*

Ben Jonson (1572/3-1637) was a dramatist, poet, scholar and author of court masques. He was born in or near London and was educated at Westminster School. Before he became well known as a writer he was employed by his stepfather as a bricklayer, and then travelled as a soldier in Flanders where he is supposed to have killed an enemy in single combat. He also joined a travelling theatre company (strolling players).

MANLEY HOPKINS, GERARD: *Inversnaid*

DID YOU KNOW?

Seamus Heaney says that Gerard Manley Hopkins is the poet who most influenced his early style.

Gerard Manley Hopkins was born in 1844 in Stratford, Essex, to a prosperous and artistic family. He was a highly intelligent young man and was educated in Highgate and at Oxford University. He had an intense interest in religion and eventually left the Church of England to join the Catholic Church in 1866. He became a Jesuit priest, destroying all the poetry he had already written, since he felt that poetry conflicted with his religious principles. However, as a student of Theology in North Wales he began to write again. His work though was so unusual that it was not published in his lifetime. After his death from typhoid in 1889 his friend, the Poet Laureate Robert Bridges, finally arranged the publication of his work in 1918. Since then his reputation has grown. Gerard Manley Hopkins is now regarded as one of the leading poets of his age.

SHAKESPEARE, WILLIAM: *Sonnet 130*

DID YOU KNOW?

William Shakespeare was a shareholder in the Globe Theatre that burnt down during a performance of his play *Henry VIII*.

William Shakespeare is one of the most famous men in history and a writer of global significance. He was born in 1564 in Stratford-upon-Avon. His family was prosperous and he probably attended the local grammar school. He married Anne Hathaway who was eight years older than him and pregnant in 1582. They were to have three children. Nothing is known about the next few years of his life, though he probably joined a travelling group of actors and left Stratford. William Shakespeare wrote 154 sonnets. Some critics believe that they represent his most personal writing. They say that they are like a diary that outlines actual events in his life.

TENNYSON, ALFRED: *Ulysses/ The Eagle*

Alfred, Lord Tennyson was the fourth of twelve children of a clergyman in Somersby, Lincolnshire. His grandfather had disinherited his father and he spent his early years in relative poverty. His life and work encompass most of the Victorian age and he is seen as one of the writers, along with Charles Dickens, who represent this time. He was a popular figure of national importance. Alfred Tennyson was very patriotic and both excited and disturbed by the great changes that were occurring in his lifetime. His poetic style was very conventional. He had an instinctive grasp of **rhythm** and the sound of his poems. They are ideally suited to being read aloud. This makes some of his best work very memorable.

TICHBORNE, CHARLES: *Elegy*

Tichborne was a Catholic who lost his life during the religious persecutions of the sixteenth century. It is likely that Tichborne was hung, drawn and quartered and his head displayed on a pole after the execution. Tichborne was made a Saint of the Catholic Church by becoming one of the 'Forty Martyrs of England and Wales'.

WHITMAN, WALT: *Patrolling Barnegat*

Walt Whitman was born near Huntington, New York, in 1819. His father was a carpenter. When Whitman was four years old, his family moved to Brooklyn, New York, and after attending school for six years he was apprenticed to a printer. He subsequently had a wide variety of jobs, including being a newspaper editor, a teacher and a builder, until he decided to devote the rest of his life to writing poetry. Whitman's poetry shows an assertion of the value of the individual and the connectedness of all humanity. It makes a defiant break with traditional poetic concerns and its style exerted a major influence on American thought and literature.

WORDSWORTH, WILLIAM: *The Affliction of Margaret*

Wordsworth was born 7 April 1770 in Cockermouth, Cumberland. His father was a steward on a country estate and the poet's childhood was relatively hard, especially since his mother died when

EXAMINER'S SECRET

You will not earn marks for regurgitating the life story of a writer.

CHECK THE NET
http://members.aol.com/wordspage/bio.htm contains a useful Wordsworth biography.

DID YOU KNOW?
An 1899 police report described Yeats as 'more or less revolutionary'. He published 'Easter 1916' in 1916 about the Irish nationalist uprising.

he was eight and his father when he was thirteen. A lonely, self-sufficient boy, it was at this time that he began to develop a fondness for the beauty and sublimity of the Lake District. Wordsworth had strong republican sympathies and was greatly influenced by the events in revolutionary France. From 1797 Wordsworth lived with his sister, Dorothy. They met the poet Samuel Taylor Coleridge, and he and Wordsworth began a collaboration that resulted in their publishing *Lyrical Ballads*.

YEATS, WILLIAM BUTLER: *The Song of the Old Mother*

William Butler Yeats was born in Dublin. His father was a lawyer and painter. In 1867 the family moved to London but returned to Dublin in 1881. Yeats studied at the Metropolitan School of Art and became interested in the supernatural and mysticism. He was also interested in folktales and participated in the movement for the revival of Celtic identity. He died in 1939.

Now take a break!

Romanticism

Wordsworth, Coleridge, Blake and Southey belonged to the first stage of the Romantic movement of poetry.

- The Romantics valued individual feelings and intuition above reason. Indeed they were individualists who spent more time disagreeing than collaborating with each other.

- They believed in imaginative freedom.

- They were interested in 'natural' forms of human existence, such as peasants, outsiders, children, whom they believed were uncorrupted by organised society.

- They had a strong sense of the importance of their own experience as a way to acquire insight and wisdom, so a lot of their writing is autobiographical.

- Above all, the Romantics thought that the contemplation of nature was a way of coming to an understanding of the self. Hence Wordsworth's attachment to Westmoreland, an area of great natural beauty, then, as it is now.

- In the preface to the *Lyrical Ballads* (1800) Wordsworth defines poetry as 'the spontaneous overflow of powerful feelings'. This meant that poems should shape themselves 'organically' rather than adhere to a set of pre-existing rules of composition. It also means that Wordsworth wanted to express himself in a more 'natural' language than conventional **poetic diction**, as he says 'a selection of language really used by men'. In this way Wordsworth established for the nineteenth and twentieth centuries the idea that poetry could be written using 'ordinary' language.

- They were greatly influenced by the events of the French Revolution and its consequences. They were revolutionary sympathizers but the Napoleonic wars made Coleridge and Wordsworth change their stance and they became conservative in their outlook.

Part Two

Summaries

Havisham

1 Miss Havisham is a character from *Great Expectations* by Charles Dickens who was jilted on the day of her wedding. She has remained a bitter recluse all her life.

2 The first verse refers to her fiancé who let her down so badly. She wants him dead.

3 In the second verse she describes herself as an unmarried woman disabled by grief and despair – 'Whole days in bed cawing Nooooo at the wall' (lines 5–6). She looks at herself in the mirror and cannot recognise who she is – 'her, myself' (line 8).

4 In the third verse she describes a psychosexual fantasy about the 'lost body' (line 10) and what she does to it.

5 The fourth verse sums up her psychological predicament: her 'honeymoon' (line 15) has become a lifetime devoted to the hatred of men and an angry lust for the corpse of her former fiancé, or indeed any man.

CHECK THE BOOK

Read *Great Expectations* by Charles Dickens and study the character of Miss Havisham. What do you think Dickens would make of Carol Anne Duffy's version of his character?

DID YOU KNOW?

The most important thing about Miss Havisham is that she is a spinster, a condition of shame in her era, but there is additional humiliation in the fact that she has been jilted on her wedding day.

Structure

The poem consists of four, four-line stanzas or **quatrains**. The first provides the reader with the theme of revenge: 'Not a day since then / I haven't wished him dead' (lines 1–2). Verses two and three develop a description of her life and state of mind. The final verse returns to the ideas of death, violent hatred and marriage: 'Give me a male corpse for a long slow honeymoon' (line 15).

Style

The poem is a dramatic **monologue**. At first the speaker appears to be addressing the man who jilted her – 'Beloved sweetheart bastard' (line 1). These three words manage to combine the ideas of both the love and hatred felt for the man. (Notice the violence of the 'b' sounds.) Yet by the end of the poem the speaker has abandoned direct address – 'a male corpse' (line 15) implies a generalised hatred of the male sex. The final line implies that even language itself has broken down for the speaker: 'Don't think its only the heart that b-b-b-breaks' (line 16).

THEMES

The poem depicts a personality in collapse, knotted up, twisted by the rejection she has experienced and her desire for revenge. In the novel, *Great Expectations*, Dickens always refers to her as *Miss* Havisham, but Duffy discards the social label *Miss* as if to concentrate the reader's attention more upon the woman's stark psychological situation. Names in the poem trace the history of her emotional life: 'beloved…sweetheart…bastard…spinster… corpse'. Duffy seems to be interested in the tortured mixture of love and hatred, because Havisham's sexual passion has not ended with her experience of rejection: 'the lost body over me, / my fluent tongue in its mouth…' (lines 10–11).

> **CHECKPOINT 1**
>
> Which image in the poem most sums up Havisham's attitude to her former lover?

> ## Links
>
> **Methods used to create a first person persona**
> - My Last Duchess (Robert Browning)
>
> **Women's position**
> - Song of the Old Mother (William Wordsworth)
>
> **Despair**
> - Tichborne's Elegy (Charles Tichborne)
>
> **Jealousy/hate**
> - The Laboratory (Robert Browning)

DID YOU KNOW?

Duffy attended two Catholic schools as a child where she says: 'They did nothing but lists, relieved only by the Latin Mass...' (quoted in the *Guardian*, Saturday August 31, 2002).

Elvis's Twin Sister

1. The twin sister of Elvis Presley, a nun, describes life in a convent.

2. The Reverend Mother, she says, likes the way she gyrates her hips.

3. She hears Gregorian chants and describes her 'simple' clothes, including a pair of blue suede shoes.

4. She thinks of her convent as being like her brother's lavish home, Graceland. This thought puts a smile on her face.

5. She is pleased she is not lonely and that she is alive and well.

STRUCTURE

In six verses we learn about Elvis Presley's imaginary twin sister. The lines are short phrases, rather like a pop lyric, and there are some **half-rhymes** – 'grow/roll' (lines 3 and 5), 'keys/shoes' (lines 18 and 20). The first four verses (lines 1–20) describe aspects of her life in the convent. The last two (lines 21–30) summarise how she feels about her life and spiritual condition.

STYLE

The poem takes the form of a song lyric, not surprisingly, and is in a

simple verse form. Duffy's lines often appear to be informal, and this type of poem suits this aspect of her style – the lines rhyme sometimes but not from any predetermined design; the pop-lyric style depends on a casual phrasing of ordinary speech – 'They call me / Sister Presley here...' (lines 6–7).

THEMES

Elvis Presley was an icon of male sexuality. In this poem his female 'twin' is imagined as the complete opposite, a chaste nun, except that, wittily, Duffy ascribes some of the qualities associated with Elvis to his holy sister – '... I move my hips / Just like my brother' (lines 9–10), '...slow lopsided smile' (line 24), 'blue suede shoes' (line 20). Clearly a comparison is intended between the two and the nurturing, peaceful female 'half' is shown as the one who has survived in 'a land of grace' (line 23) where she is 'alive and well' (line 27). If Elvis Presley was at one time an idol and an ideal, what kind of a woman is his twin sister?

The **epigraphs** at the head of the poem give a clue to its themes: can you work out the connection between the first one (a quotation from a famous Elvis song) and the meaning of the last verse? Equally, the quotation from Madonna should give rise to reflections on the issues of gender that crop up in Duffy's poems generally.

DID YOU KNOW?

Elvis Presley had a hit in 1956 with a song called 'Blue Suede Shoes'.

EXAMINER'S SECRET

It would be a good idea to list the features of the poem that indicate it is written from a female perspective.

CHECKPOINT 2

How does the imagery used in **'The Laboratory'** (strong and sensuous) compare to that used by Duffy?

Links

Contented attitude to life

- Sonnet (John Clare)

Different situations of two women

- Song of the Old Mother (W. B. Yeats)

A first-person narrator

- My Last Duchess (Robert Browning)
- The Laboratory (Robert Browning)

Anne Hathaway

1. Shakespeare's widow, Anne Hathaway, describes the 'next best bed' (line 14) and what it means to her.

2. She compares the bed they shared to the world of Shakespeare's imagination.

3. Their lovemaking in the bed is compared to his language-making.

4. Sometimes, she recalls, she would dream that she herself was one of her husband's imaginative creations ('he'd written me', line 8) and that all his poetic dramas originated in their intimacy.

5. In the guestroom their guests slept upon the best bed 'dribbling ... prose' (line 12).

6. Now she keeps the memory of her love alive as firmly as he held her upon the bed.

STRUCTURE

The poem is in Shakespearean **sonnet** form, fourteen lines made up of three **quatrains** and a **couplet**. Unlike the classic form this particular sonnet does not employ strict rhymes except in the couplet.

STYLE

Shakespeare's widow is characterised as a passionate, loving woman who had privileged access to one of the most creative minds ever. There are echoes of Shakespeare's own writing (such as 'The barge she sat in' from *Antony and Cleopatra*), of the imaginative locations of his plays, e.g. The forest of Arden, Denmark, the sea, but the central idea or **conceit** is the comparison between the act of poetic literary creation and the physical act of love.

THEMES

Carol Ann Duffy has spoken of the almost erotic aspect to writing poetry and here she seems to be trying to describe what this idea means within a classic form of love poetry, the sonnet. There are references to the heightened emotions of sexual love – 'spinning world' (line 1), 'shooting stars' (line 14), and the use of writing/language as a **metaphor** for lovemaking – 'his touch / a verb dancing in the centre of a noun' (lines 6/7).

> ### CHECKPOINT 3
> Why do you think Anne Hathaway writes in sonnet form?

Links

Male/female relationship, writing
- Sonnet 130 (William Shakespeare)

Male/female – effect of touch
- My Last Duchess (Robert Browning)

Different type of love
- Sonnet (John Clare)

> **EXAMINER'S SECRET**
> It would be useful to examine how Duffy and Clare differ in their use of the sonnet form.

Salome

1 Salome recalls waking up with a head on her pillow and wondering whose it is.

2 She called for her maid to bring her some breakfast and started to feel better.

③ **She vows to give up 'the booze, fags and the sex' (line 27).**

④ **She pulls back the bloody bedclothes and reveals the severed head on a platter.**

STRUCTURE

Salome is in four verses that reflect a simple structure.

- The first establishes the situation – Salome's reflections on her habit of waking to find the head of a man on her pillow. Questions about the possible name of the present 'head' link verse one with the next.

- The second verse describes how she started to feel less 'hungover' when the maid brought in her breakfast.

- The third verse deals with her resolve to give up this dissolute life of '…the booze and the fags and the sex' (line 27). She decides to 'turf out the blighter' (line 29) from her bed.

- A final short verse of four lines provides the climax: pulling back the sheets she reveals his bloodied head 'on a platter' (line 36).

STYLE

The poem is written in a distinctive colloquial manner – 'booze and the fags and the sex' (line 27), 'wrecked' (line 23) – that gives it a chatty, anecdotal tone. There are several '-er' ending rhymes, adding to the sense of a flow of language casually put together yet culminating in the key final word, 'platter'. The first line – 'I'd done it before' – plunges the reader into an ongoing conversation, as if Salome has been explaining herself to a friend. The verb tenses place the events into a phase of the past that has been completed. There are some effective **alliterations** in the second verse, lines 18–19, where the sound of the maid's activity sharpens Salome's 'hungover' brain. The tone of the poem throughout is frivolous ('and ain't life a bitch', line 35), that of a superficial young girl who is spoiled and self-indulgent.

THEMES

The legend of 'Salome' derives from a sparse Biblical account of the step-daughter of Herod, Tetrach of Judea, and her shocking insistence upon the beheading of St John the Baptist. In the original Gospel story, Salome was depicted as an amoral adolescent who is told by her aggrieved mother, Herodias, to demand the prophet's head on a platter. The story has been popular with artists and writers, especially at the end of the nineteenth century.

Links

Confession of a woman

- The Laboratory
  (Robert Browning)

Recreation of mythological character

- Ulysses
  (Alfred Tennyson)

Contrast of women's occupations

- The Affliction of Margaret
  (William Wordsworth)

Use of imagery

- Patrolling Barnegat
  (Walt Whitman)

CHECKPOINT 4

What other poem by Duffy could you link with **'Salome'**?

 CHECK THE NET

Search the Internet for other depictions of 'Salome'.

Before You Were Mine

1 The poet is looking at a photograph of her mother as a teenager, ten years before she was born.

2 She describes how her mother is laughing with two of her friends.

3 She realises that this is a part of her mother's life before she even thought of having a child. Her mother, like all teenagers, was devoted to having a good time.

4 The poet thinks back to her own childhood and how she used to play with her mother's red shoes. Perhaps her mother wore them in George Square when out on a date.

5 She remembers how her mother used to try and teach her the *cha cha* steps in the street. She wished she could have known her mother then, when she was so young and carefree (before she became a mother).

? **DID YOU KNOW?**

Marilyn Monroe died of a drug overdose in 1962 and never became a mother.

STRUCTURE

The poem is written in four equal verses of five lines each. It is structured around different phases in time:

- There are references to the ten years before the poet was born, and these, like the regularity of the verses, may remind the reader of the way time passes as the pages of a photograph album are being turned

- The time when the poet was a little girl

- The present, when the poet is remembering and thinking about her mother

You should identify the relevant references to these three stages. What do you think is the poet's attitude towards her mother in each one?

STYLE

Pick out the references to her mother – 'you laugh…and shriek at the pavement' (lines 1 and 4), 'the bold girl winking in Portobello' (line 18), 'you sparkle and waltz and laugh' (line 20) – and consider why Duffy presents her mother's life as happy and 'glamorous' (line 19). She links her to her famous namesake, Marilyn Monroe, and makes a contrast between her mother's life as a young girl and her life as the mother of Carol Ann. What does the phrase 'loud, possessive yell' (line 11) tell you about the relationship between mother and daughter?

The present tense is used throughout the poem. What effect does this have on the way you understand it? How does it make you read the account of past experiences?

The **tone** of the poet's voice is very strong and confident. She has written as if she is talking to her mother in the present and has a certain knowingness about her mother's feelings – 'The decade ahead…was the best one, eh?' (line 11). The poem is addressed to her mother, yet seems to be more about the poet herself. What do you think contributes to this effect?

THEMES

There are many types of love and by writing a kind of love poem about her mother, Duffy shows yet again another aspect of her originality. Memory and the passing of time are themes of several other poems in *Mean Time* (1993).

CHECKPOINT 5

Why do you think the name 'Marilyn' (line 5) is a one-word sentence?

 DID YOU KNOW?

The word 'possessive' (line 11) is unusual. It would be more normal for a parent to be possessive about a child, but Duffy turns this idea around to make the mother *belong* to the child.

Links

Uses of vivid imagery
- Patrolling Barnegat (Walt Whitman)
- Ulysses (Alfred Tennyson)

Relationship between mother and child
- Mother, any distance (Simon Armitage)

? DID YOU KNOW?

The situation of *We Remember Your Childhood Well* resembles a psychological condition known as 'False Memory Syndrome'. But whose memory is 'false'?

We Remember Your Childhood Well

❶ In this poem, the persona, who could be a parent figure, addresses a person about their childhood experiences.

❷ Each stanza provides 'corrected' versions of a series of unhappy memories which have been implicitly brought up by the addressee.

STRUCTURE

Six three-line verses in **free verse** style. The poem hangs upon four strategically placed sentences: 'Nobody hurt you' (line 1), 'Nobody forced you' (line 7), 'Nobody sent you away' (line 13), 'We remember your childhood well' (line 18). This is the bare argument of the speaker.

STYLE

The speaker of this poem will be familiar to anyone who has had painful childhood experiences that their parents will not accept or take responsibility for. Duffy brings together a collection of typical incidents which are intended to characterise all the most fearful things that can happen to a child: the light turned off, adults arguing all night, the 'bad man' (line 2), a locked door, being sent away.

Written in conversational style, with simple **diction** and **syntax**, the poem builds up to a climax at the fourth verse: 'We called the tune. / The secret police of your childhood were older and wiser than you' (lines 10–11). The voice is assertive throughout, but here a new tone comes into play. 'The secret police' is a term that the notional speaker probably would not use because it is loaded with negative **connotations.** Why do you think Duffy breaks away from the 'realistic' **register** here? Notice the way 'Boom' (line 12) echoes 'tune' (line 10) in this verse. What effect do you think is intended?

You might like to consider the phrase 'the skidmarks of sin / on your soul and laid you wide open for Hell' (lines 16–17), not only in terms of register, but as a clue to what really happened during this unhappy childhood. What might be the child's version of his/her childhood? What other clues in the poem imply a **subtext?**

THEMES

This **monologue** dramatises the denial of a child's memories. The theme of memory is common in Duffy's poetry. As in other poems, Duffy is using the **dramatic monologue** form to give a sense of the unreliability of language, its use as an instrument of power and coercion. The poem contains some **ambiguity.** Try to identify words and phrases that could be carrying other meanings.

EXAMINER'S SECRET
Go through the poems by themes and make your own short list. Note what makes them *similar* (language, structure, attitudes, ideas, feelings) and then take careful note of what makes them different.

Links

Childhood fears

- Little Boy Lost/Found (William Blake)

Summation of a life

- Tichborne's Elegy (Charles Tichborne)

Dramatic monologue that creates a sense of threat

- The Laboratory (Robert Browning)

Education for Leisure

❶ The persona in the poem decides he is going to kill someone. He's fed up 'of being ignored' (line 2) and wants 'to play God' (line 3).

CHECK THE NET

A great Carol Ann Duffy site is **http://www.geocities.com/klf67/duffy.html**

2 He squashes a fly against the window pane and remembers doing Shakespeare at school.

3 He believes he is a 'genius' (line 9) and could do anything if he wanted to. He thinks that this is the day when he is 'going to change the world' (line 10).

4 He pours the goldfish down the lavatory. He says that he has to walk two miles every fortnight to sign on and 'They don't appreciate my autograph' (line 16).

5 There is nothing left to kill in the house. He phones up a radio show and 'tells the man he's talking to a superstar' (line 18). He picks up the bread-knife and goes out into the street.

STRUCTURE

The first stanza provides the motive for the persona's actions – 'I have had enough of being ignored and today / I am going to play God' (lines 2–3). The poem dramatises his thoughts and actions just before he goes out to kill someone, each stanza taking the reader closer to the fateful last sentence 'I touch your arm' (line 20).

STYLE

The title sounds like some sort of government-inspired education initiative. It is obviously **ironic**. This character, like other loners and misfits whose voices Duffy has adopted, has clearly had a pointless education ('Shakespeare. It was in / another language', lines 6–7) and his leisure time is an endlessly bleak stretch of unemployment ('...I walk the two miles into town / for signing on', lines 15–16). What he has learned, however, is the basic lesson of psychopaths: the only way to feel powerful and important is to go out and kill something.

DID YOU KNOW?

It is easy to assume the speaker is male even though nothing explicitly tells us this is the case. Why?

The repetition of 'I' throughout gives the poem a tight, claustrophobic feeling, as of the character trapped inside his deluded sense of self. The present tense reinforces the idea that this person lives as if he has neither a past nor a future, his only concern is the immediate impulses that have to be gratified.

Language or writing are referred to quite a lot in this poem. What point do you think is being made by this? The character thinks he is a 'genius' yet he only destroys.

THEMES

Like 'Stealing' this poem concerns an individual who resorts to criminal acts. Duffy gives the character a chance to gain the reader's understanding, if not complete sympathy, and reminds us that this character is connected to us by the chilling final sentence 'I touch your arm' (line 20).

Links

A first-person persona

- My Last Duchess
  (Robert Browning)

- The Laboratory
  (Robert Browning)

- Hitcher
  (Simon Armitage)

DID YOU KNOW?

There is a **satirical** aspect to the poem: ('The cat avoids me. The cat / knows I am a genius', lines 11–12).

CHECKPOINT 6

Which Shakespeare play does this come from: 'As flies to wanton boys are we to the Gods'? How might it apply to the character in the poem?

Stealing

❶ A burglar and petty thief talks about the things he steals, in particular a snowman 'a tall, white mute / beneath the winter moon' (lines 2–3).

❷ The snowman was cold and heavy but 'part of the thrill was knowing / that children would cry in the morning' (lines 9–10).

❸ The burglar describes how he steals for the sake of it, or breaks into houses 'just to have a look' (line 12).

❹ When he tried to reassemble the snowman in his backyard it didn't look the same so he destroyed it.

❺ The speaker describes how bored he is. He has stolen a guitar and a bust of Shakespeare, but 'the snowman was strangest' (line 24).

DID YOU KNOW?

As in '**Education for Leisure**' it is easy to assume the thief is male. Is this sexist? Is this justified?

STRUCTURE

This **dramatic monologue** is organised into five stanzas of regular length. The questions to an implied listener in the first and last line give a frame to the speech. Stanzas three and five contain digressions from the story of the snowman, which add to the effect of an informal conversation.

EXAMINER'S SECRET

Alliteration can emphasise important words. Look up some examples in the poem and note their effect.

STYLE

The informal **register** of the speaker provides a convincing sense of the character – 'I'm a mucky ghost' (line 13), 'I nicked a bust of Shakespeare once, / flogged it' (lines 23–4). The complete pointlessness of what the man does is shown in such details as 'I joy-ride cars / to nowhere' (lines 11–12).

Internal rhyme is used to develop the interior exploration of the man's motives – 'the slice of ice / within my own brain' (lines 4–5) indicates some self-knowledge in the character, a cold person who cannot empathise. This idea is reinforced in the second stanza in the rhymes 'chill' (line 8) and 'thrill' (line 9). Clearly the snowman is an appropriate 'mate' (line 3) for the thief; it is an object that is both unfeeling and conveniently 'mute' (line 2).

THEMES

What kind of a person would steal a snowman? Apparently this poem originated in an actual event. When Carol Ann Duffy was living in London her neighbours built a traditional snowman and it was stolen. Apart from attempting to explore the individual psychology of the thief, Duffy makes his attitudes and actions stand for a wider set of values that she thinks exist in society.

- What do you understand by the thief's philosophy as expressed at the start of stanza two: 'Better off dead than giving in, not taking / what you want' (lines 6–7)?

- What attracts the thief to the snowman in the first place and why does he destroy it?

- What have the snowman, the guitar and the bust of Shakespeare got in common?

Links

The first person

- The Hitcher (Simon Armitage)

The ways in which a persona can reveal psychology and motive

- My Last Duchess (Robert Browning)
- Ulysses (Alfred Tennyson)

EXAMINER'S SECRET

Think about what the last line of the poem tells us about the thief.

CHECK THE BOOK

Look up other examples of Duffy's explorations of unstable characters: *Psychopath* (Selling Manhattan) and *Liar* (The Other Country).

Now take a break!

TEST YOURSELF (CAROL ANN DUFFY)

FROM WHICH POEM?

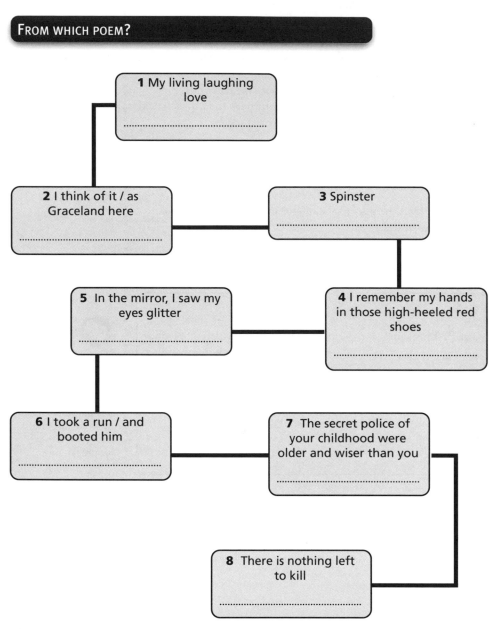

1 My living laughing love

....

2 I think of it / as Graceland here

....

3 Spinster

....

5 In the mirror, I saw my eyes glitter

....

4 I remember my hands in those high-heeled red shoes

....

6 I took a run / and booted him

....

7 The secret police of your childhood were older and wiser than you

....

8 There is nothing left to kill

....

Check your answers on p. 130.

Mother, any distance

❶ The poet's mother is helping him measure up a new home.

❷ The first stanza describes the situation: 'You come to help me measure windows, pelmets, doors' (line 3).

❸ His mother remains downstairs holding the 'zero end' (line 5) of the tape measure, while the poet takes the tape upstairs, 'unreeling / years between us' (lines 7–8).

❹ The longer final stanza describes the poet moving with the tape measure upstairs, through the empty bedroom and up to the loft, 'where something / has to give' (lines 10–11).

❺ He imagines his mother below, still holding on to the tape with her fingertips, while he reaches the hatch in the roof 'that opens on an endless sky / to fall or fly' (lines 14–15).

STRUCTURE

The poem has a natural structure of three parts, the three stanzas corresponding to:

- Mother arriving to help measure and son explaining

- Mother given tape measure to hold

- Son taking other end of tape and ascending upstairs

The first two verses are **quatrains** with **rhymes**. The third verse is longer and in **free verse** style, a single sentence 'unwinding' towards a final rhyme – 'sky', 'fly' (lines 14–15). The poem is a variation on the **sonnet** form.

STYLE

Part of Armitage's genius as a poet is his ability to combine formal qualities with a **colloquial register**. In this poem he uses the **rhythms** of everyday speech patterns – 'you at the zero-end, me with the spool of tape' (line 5), **rhyming couplets** (lines 3–4) and **metaphors** – 'the acres of the walls, the prairies of the floors' (line 4).

- Why do you think five '-ing' ending words appear in the second verse?

DID YOU KNOW?

The sonnet (Italian for 'little song') probably originated in Sicily in the thirteenth century. Petrarch, in about 1335, in a sequence dedicated to his love for an ideal woman called Laura, published the first important sonnets.

EXAMINER'S SECRET

Make a list of all the words or phrases in the poem that could have a **metaphorical** meaning. Do they indicate anything about the kind of relationship the poet has with his mother and how he regards her role in his life?

CHECKPOINT 7

Simon Armitage likes to play with the different meanings of words, which gives his poetry a certain **ambiguity,** and perhaps also reflects his dislike of fixed interpretations to his poems. Look for some evidence of ambiguity in this poem.

Aspects of the relationship between mother and son are suggested by certain words and phrases. The word 'span', for instance, in line 1 connotes the phrase *spanning the generations,* an idea which is taken up at lines 7–8 – 'unreeling / years between us'

THEMES

The poem could be read on two levels:

- A literal level, which describes an ordinary domestic task

Or

- A **metaphorical** level in which the ordinary activities stand for something else.

You might like to consider how certain **images** contribute to the idea of a powerful bond between mother and child being stretched to 'breaking point' (line 10) by the narrator's desire for freedom and independence.

Links

Motherhood/domestic tasks

- Song of the Old Mother (W. B. Yeats)

Parent/child bonds

- On my first Sonne (Ben Jonson)
- Affliction of Margaret (William Wordsworth)

My father thought it bloody queer

❶ The twenty-nine-year-old poet recalls how his father reacted when he came home with his ear pierced.

❷ He describes how they had used a jeweller's gun to make the hole and how the hole 'became a wound, and wept' (line 11).

3 Now he is twenty-nine, the poet is not surprised to hear his own voice repeating what his father had said to him: *'If I were you, / I'd take it out and leave it out next year'* (lines 14–15).

STRUCTURE

Like the previous poem this has a three-part structure. The first two stanzas establish the situation, the past event. The last stanza brings the reader up to the present and the poet's description of what this event now means to him. Again, this poem is a variation on the **sonnet** form.

STYLE

Even though the language is strongly **colloquial,** the basic ingredients of a conventional poetic style are present:

- Both **half-** and **full-rhyme** are used, the first stanza containing, appropriately, some strong **masculine rhymes.**

- **Assonance**: this is when two words sound similar because they share a vowel sound – 'rolled home' (line 2), 'cried'/'spiral' (line 14).

- **Alliteration**: several words repeat the same **consonant** – 'half hidden by a mop of hair. "You've lost your head"' (line 3), 'sleeper … slept … sore' (lines 10–11) etc. Along with rhyme

EXAMINER'S SECRET

It's not enough to just point out examples of rhyme, assonance, alliteration etc. You must be prepared to explain their particular effect in terms of meaning and sound.

DID YOU KNOW?

There is ambiguity in the phrase 'breaking like a tear' (line 13). What do you think his attitude to his father is now that he is a man?

CHECKPOINT 8

How does Armitage characterise his parents in 'Mother, any distance' and 'My father thought it bloody queer'?

and assonance, this has the effect of emphasising key words while binding the words together in a kind of musical phrase.

THEMES

Like the previous poems, simple language masks emotional and intellectual attitudes that are often complex. On the surface the poem seems humorous – 'bloody queer' (line 1) sums up the down-to-earth father's attitude in more ways than one! But in the recollection of his adolescent self there is also pain, both physical and emotional.

Links

Parent's attitude to child

- On my first Sonne (Ben Jonson)

Sonnet uses and variations, rhyme, repetition

- Anne Hathaway (Carol Ann Duffy)
- Sonnet 130 (William Shakespeare)
- Sonnet (John Clare)

Homecoming

1. The poet invites the addressee, probably a young woman, to consider two separate things at once: a trust exercise in which a person falls backwards to be caught by someone standing behind; and the 'canary-yellow cotton jacket' (line 5) that she wore as a teenager, which is depicted lying, dirtied, on the floor of a cloakroom.

2. When she returns home her mother jumps to all the wrong conclusions and they have an argument. The girl goes to bed.

3. At midnight she sneaks out of the house to make a phone call. When she returns she encounters her father, 'a father figure' (line 17), waiting at the garden gate.

4 The last verse brings the trust exercise and the jacket together – her body is compared to the different parts of the jacket and the poet invites the woman to 'Step backwards into it' (line 21) because 'It still fits' (line 23).

STRUCTURE

The first stanza introduces the idea of trusting someone. The story of the yellow jacket is given in the second stanza. The third stanza connects the poet with the young woman – 'I'm waiting by the phone, although it doesn't ring / because it's sixteen years or so before we'll meet' (lines 14–15). The final verse resolves the two elements introduced at the start, bringing the reader to the present.

STYLE

Armitage likes to use catchphrases and **idioms** in his poetry, often slightly changing them so that they contain an extra meaning. In this poem, for example, *Put two and two together and made five* becomes 'makes a proper fist of it' (line 9), which gives a strong image of the mother's anger. There are several examples of catchphrases and idioms in this poem. They add to the humour, accessibility and energy of the writing. Try to identify them and to explain how Armitage gives them a striking 'beat' through **rhythm** and repetition. You might also like to consider the role of **half-rhymes** and **enjambment**, especially in the way they contribute towards the poem's narrative elements.

THEMES

A key idea in this poem might be 'trust' (line 2). The speaker invites the person to 'Step backwards into it' (line 21), thus linking the trust exercise described in the first stanza with putting on the jacket again. What does the yellow jacket represent? Remember that this account of a past experience is the poet's and not the person addressed. You should consider the characters in the poem and how they each relate to the subject:

- The mother – 'the very model of a model of a mother' (line 8)
- The father – 'in silhouette / a father figure waits there, wants to set things straight' (lines 16–17)

DID YOU KNOW?

The final stanza contains some interesting and unconventional **metaphors** where ribs, arms, fingers and hands are compared to different parts of the jacket.

DID YOU KNOW?

Simon Armitage takes a very disciplined approach to the making of a poem: 'I prefer order to chaos and I find the structured and organised poem easier to read and easier to write' (Interview in *Verse*, Vol. 8, Number 1).

CHECKPOINT 9

Why do you think this poem is titled 'Homecoming'?

- The poet/speaker – 'I'm waiting by the phone...' (line 14)

It is easy to assume that the subject of the poem is female even though this is not explicitly stated. Why?

Links

Mother/father/child attitudes

- Little Boy Lost/Found (William Blake)

How past and present is conveyed

- Ulysses (Alfred Tennyson)

Different parent/child relationships

- The Affliction of Margaret (William Wordsworth)

November

1. The poet helps his friend take his grandma into a hospital ward.
2. They settle her down with her few possessions and leave.
3. The poet reflects that he and his friend will also become, in time, old and decrepit.
4. They drive home exhausted and depressed.

STRUCTURE

Each of the short three-line stanzas depicts a stage in the process of taking the old lady into the hospital and leaving her there.

The final **couplet**, standing as a single verse, acts to summarise the experience for the participants and the reader.

STYLE

Notice the word-play of 'It is time' (line 7), implying not only time to leave the hospital and grandma to her fate, but also the time which we are also subject to – 'and in us John' (line 9) – and which makes us 'almost these monsters' (line 9). The repetition of the word 'we' in the first stanza and elsewhere in the poem anticipates this sense of inclusiveness. Notice the positioning of the words 'your grandma' (line 2) and 'our two' (line 2) in the second line. What does 'our two' sound like?

As usual, the diction is simple, but what effect do you think the multi-syllable word 'incontinence' has at the end of the second stanza?

The poem is addressed to a specifically named character, John. This provides a sense of realism. Yet do you believe the event actually happened involving Simon Armitage and his friend John?

THEMES

The title gives the poem a context and also an indication of its theme. Notice how the idea of life coming to an end is taken up by the dusk image on line 13. The final couplet plays with the paradox of how in spite of the fact that we are going to die, 'we feel alive' (line 16) when the sun shines.

 EXAMINER'S SECRET

When writing about poems which use a **first-person narrator** be sure you distinguish between the narrator and the poet who wrote the poem – they are not the same!

CHECKPOINT 10

What effect do you think was intended by the word 'spangles' (line 16)?

DID YOU KNOW?

Armitage has said that he lifted the last line of this poem from a 1970s cowboy series *Alias Smith and Jones*. How might a piece of information like this change the way you read the poem?

Links

Attitudes to death

- Tichborne's Elegy (Charles Tichborne)
- The Man He Killed (Thomas Hardy)

Symbols of age and death

- Ulysses (Alfred Tennyson)

Kid

1. Robin has grown up and is free of Batman.

2. After Batman 'ditched' (line 4) him Robin told everybody what Batman was really like.

3. Robin does not wear his silly childish uniform any more: he now wears jeans and a crew-neck sweater. He is older and stronger now.

4. Robin imagines Batman's miserable life now that he has lost his 'shadow' (line 20).

5. Now Robin is the 'real boy wonder' (line 24).

STRUCTURE

A single stanza made up of twelve **rhyming couplets**, rhyming the same '-er' ending using mostly **half-rhymes**

The poem can be divided into three parts:

- Lines 1 to 5 describes the past event.

- Lines 6 to 18 describes Robin's present state.

- Lines 19 to 24 gives the effect this has had on Batman, at least in Robin's imagination – 'Batman, it makes a marvellous picture' (line 19).

STYLE

The powerful emotions of the speaker have created complex sound patterns throughout this poem, in spite of the apparently simple idea of a repeating '-er' sound. Read the poem aloud first and try out different tones of voice to enable you to explore the emotions. Notice:

- The explosive **alliteration** in the first line

- The use of sarcastic **cliché** – 'the wild blue yonder' (line 3), 'he was like a father / to me' (lines 6–7)

- The outraged **tabloidese** of 'Holy robin-redbreast-nest-egg-shocker!' (line 12)

- The hard emphasis in the repetition of 'now I'm taller, harder, stronger, older' (line 18)

- The use of **enjambment** to accommodate the teeming speech of the speaker

THEMES

Robin's dislike and resentment of Batman reflects a wide variety of domestic and family situations. Why do you think Armitage used comic-book characters to embody this theme?

CHECK THE BOOK

'Kid' is the title poem from Armitage's second book of poems. The book includes several poems with themes of domestic tension, law and order, submerged and exploding violence, and the anarchic strain in the human psyche.

Those bastards in their mansions

❶ The poet/speaker mocks the way 'Those bastards in their mansions' (line 1) regard him with horror.

❷ Anybody would think he had stormed into their homes and robbed them of 'the gift of fire' (line 6) and then gone to the ordinary people and set them free and armed them.

❸ The 'lords and ladies' (line 10) would have the poet killed.

❹ He stays in the shadows carrying a gun.

EXAMINER'S SECRET

Don't be afraid to make your own interpretations when writing about poems. You will **not** be rewarded for reciting your teacher's opinions!

STRUCTURE

Like all the poems from *The Book of Matches* sequence this is a variation on the **sonnet** form. The four sections are not regular; they show different stages of the ideas in the poem. The whole poem seems to be held together by strong active verbs – 'poisoned', 'vaulted', 'crossed', 'forced', 'lifted', 'armed', 'sniffed', 'picked', 'pinned', 'grilled'. Repetition and **rhyme** are also used to add to the sense of energy and threat that pervades throughout. The final line is separated from the rest of the poem to give it some emphasis.

STYLE

In this poem Armitage has used a variety of **stereotypes** from the age of proletarian revolution in the eighteenth and nineteenth centuries and linked them to the myth of Prometheus. Try to identify the received images, such as 'poisoned the dogs and vaulted the ditches' (line 3) and reflect on the effect intended. Are they supposed to be funny in some way? Armitage's poems often have an accessibly humorous tone combined with a **colloquial** realism and critical seriousness. What serious point might he be making in this poem? He has adopted a **first-person persona**: is he identifying with Prometheus? If so, what might be the poet Armitage's 'gift of fire' (line 6) and why might it threaten the 'lords and ladies in their palaces and castles' (line 10)?

THEMES

- The final line is a paraphrase of a favourite proverb which President Theodore Roosevelt (President of USA 1901–09) liked to quote, 'Speak softly and carry a big stick ...', made when he was steering the United States towards a more active role in world politics.

- Throughout history, Prometheus has symbolized unyielding strength that resists oppression.

How might these two facts point to a possible theme for this poem?

Links

Sonnet uses and variations

- Sonnet 130
  (William Shakespeare)
- Sonnet
  (John Clare)

Methods to create first-person persona

- Havisham
  (Carol Ann Duffy)
- My Last Duchess
  (Robert Browning)

 DID YOU KNOW?

Prometheus sneaked into Olympus at night and made his way to the Chariot of the Sun and lit a torch from the fires that burned there. Extinguishing the torch, Prometheus carried the still hot coals down the mountain. Upon reaching the Lands of Men, Prometheus gave to them the coals, breaking Zeus's order by giving fire to Man. Zeus ordered that Prometheus be chained to a rock where his torture was to be carried out. Every day a great eagle would come to Prometheus and eat his liver, leaving only at nightfall when the liver would begin to grow back once more, only to repeat the process again the next day.

I've made out a will

1 The poet/speaker has decided to leave the internal organs of his body to the National Health Service.

2 They can have everything except his heart.

3 His heart will be left 'where it stops or hangs' (line 15).

STRUCTURE

Another **sonnet** from *The Book of Matches*, which employs one of Armitage's favoured devices, the list. This is woven into the simple grammatical structure of *They can use this but not that.* The first part of this structure – *They can use this* – builds up an extraordinary variety of **metaphors** over twelve lines; the second part is simply a separated **couplet** providing the conclusion of the argument.

STYLE

The inventory of body parts that makes up this poem reads like an exploration of the possibilities of poetic comparison. This kind of descriptive device has its literary origin in the **blazon** used by Elizabethan poets in their love sonnets, where they would often

? DID YOU KNOW?
The form of the poem takes some aspects of both the traditional **Italian sonnet** and the **Shakespearean sonnet**: the first eight lines reflect the **octave** of the former; then from line 9 to line 14 there is the **quatrain** and final **couplet** from the latter.

praise a woman's beauty by listing her external physical qualities. By writing about himself when he will be dead and by using his largely *internal* organs, Armitage has transformed this traditional method into something very different. One thing does remain from the traditional love sonnet, however: the heart. What effect does this have on the way you read the poem? Why is the heart the one thing he won't leave to the National Health?

'The loops and coils and sprockets and springs and rods' (line 10) compare the poet's body to a mechanical machine, a clock, a word that is echoed by 'stock' in line 9. Try to identify all the different types of 'stock' referred to in the first 8 lines. The images have strong **connotations**. For example, in what ways can the skeleton, the bones of the body, be a 'chassis or cage or cathedral' (line 7)? What does 'the loaf of brains' (line 4) make you think of?

THEMES

The body is a material thing; the essence of a person's feelings is often symbolised by the heart. In one sense the poem is about the author's body, but it also forces us to consider what his heart means to him as a symbol.

> **CHECKPOINT 11**
>
> Is the final line – 'leave that where it stops or hangs' – an acknowledgement that this is the part of him that cannot be touched or used by the world?

Links

Reflections on death and preparation for death

- Tichborne's Elegy (Charles Tichborne)
- Ulysses (Alfred Tennyson)

Imagery

- Patrolling Barnegat (Walt Whitman)

Sonnet uses and variations

- Havisham (Carol Ann Duffy)
- Sonnet 130 (William Shakespeare)
- Sonnet (John Clare)

Hitcher

1. The persona, a frustrated worker, is on his way to work in a hired Vauxhall Astra.

2. He recounts how he picked up a hitchhiker in Leeds.

3. The hitcher told him about his philosophy of life.

4. The speaker describes how he attacked the hitcher with the krooklok while still driving the car.

5. He pushed the hitcher out of the car.

DID YOU KNOW?

We should ask ourselves whether we can trust a narrator's version of events! Think about 'The Laboratory' (Robert Browning).

STRUCTURE

The five stanzas have a regular five-line shape with the third line being the longest in each. The visual shape of the stanzas is interesting. The third line seems to push outwards to a point of climax, making the stanzas arrow-shaped. Look at the final word of each third line and see if you can see how these words might constitute a key element in each stanza, or put together in sequence reflect on the theme of the poem generally.

STYLE

The style brings together the formality of Simon Armitage's writing and his use of **vernacular** speech ('under/the weather' lines 1–2).

The first stanza contains some typical **internal rhymes**, which serve to bind the lines together – 'tired', 'fired', 'hired'. Think about how these musical effects relate to the persona's state of mind at the start.

Clichés are used extensively in the poem, especially in the reported words of the hitcher: 'The truth, / he said, was blowin' in the wind, / or round the next bend' (lines 8–10), 'He'd said he liked the breeze / to run its fingers / through his hair' (lines 20–2).

This should give you some idea of the type of person he is, and the differences between him and the speaker. But how can you deduce the speaker's attitude towards him from this speech?

THEMES

The poem appears to be about an act of casual violence. But can you guess the speaker's motives from his description of the hitcher? Remember that a hitcher is someone who wants a free ride.

> **EXAMINER'S SECRET**
> **'Hitcher'** is a **dramatic monologue,** thus it only provides the reader with partial information about the events described. Think about the event from the point of view of a neutral observer.

Links

Methods to create the first person

- The Song of the Old Mother (W. B. Yeats)
- The Laboratory (Robert Browning)
- Ulysses (Alfred Tennyson)

Casual random violence

- Education for Leisure (Carol Ann Duffy)
- The Man He Killed (Thomas Hardy)

> **EXAMINER'S SECRET**
> Always refer to details of particular relevance to the question in your answers. Generalisations will not earn many marks.

Now take a break!

FROM WHICH POEM?

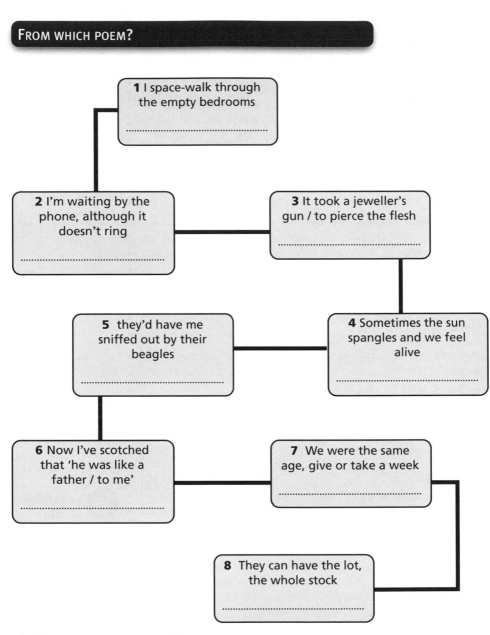

1 I space-walk through the empty bedrooms

....

2 I'm waiting by the phone, although it doesn't ring

....

3 It took a jeweller's gun / to pierce the flesh

....

5 they'd have me sniffed out by their beagles

....

4 Sometimes the sun spangles and we feel alive

....

6 Now I've scotched that 'he was like a father / to me'

....

7 We were the same age, give or take a week

....

8 They can have the lot, the whole stock

....

Check your answers on p. 130.

BEN JONSON, 1616 – On my first Sonne

1. The poet bids farewell to his seven-year-old son who has died.

2. He feels that he has is being punished for expecting too much of the boy.

3. He wishes that he could cease to feel as a father and wonders why people lament the dead when they should be envied.

4. At least his son, having died so young, has avoided all the misery that life can bring.

5. He bids his son rest peacefully. The boy will be known as Ben Jonson's best piece of poetry.

6. From now on, Jonson will never become too attached to anything he loves.

 DID YOU KNOW?
Jonson was tried at the Old Bailey for murder for killing fellow actor, Gabriel Spencer, in a dual in the Fields at Shoreditch. He escaped the gallows only by pleading benefit of clergy.

STRUCTURE

The poem is an **epitaph**, or **elegy**, which was a common poetic form in Jonson's time.

There are twelve lines of **rhyming couplets** divided into three sections.

 DID YOU KNOW?
Wordsworth wrote three essays on epitaphs. Yeats actually composed his own epitaph at the end of his poem 'Under Ben Bulben'.

DID YOU KNOW?

Ben Jonson is believed by some – wrongly of course – to be the real author of Shakespeare's plays.

In the first four lines, after the poet has bid his son farewell, he tries to find some meaning for his loss. These lines promote the idea that the boy's death is somehow the result of Jonson's pride, his possessive ambition for his son's future. The child had only been 'lent' (line 3) and after seven years it was time to 'pay' him back.

In the next four lines Jonson questions his own grief. He asks why we should lament the enviable state of death when the child has escaped suffering and the misery of ageing. He cannot answer this question.

The final four lines resolve the situation. He asks that the child, or perhaps the maker of the gravestone, record that this boy was Jonson's 'best piece of poetrie' (line 10), his proudest creation. He concludes by vowing that he will be more careful with those he loves; wary of liking and so needing them too much.

STYLE

Jonson's poetic language can be described as strong and vigorous, virile. Read the poem aloud in the voice you think Jonson might have used – phrases such as 'O, could I lose all Father, now' (line 5) have a directness and emotional honesty that are very typical of the poet. There is no elaborate **imagery**; the **metaphor** of the boy's life as a loan – 'Seven yeeres tho' wert lent to me, and I thee pay...' (line 3) is simple and everyday.

This style or **tone** of writing owes much to the Latin classical poets: Catullus, Martial, Horace, while at the same time it is not far removed from colloquial English.

CHECKPOINT 12

Which of the two modern poets you are studying comes closest to Jonson in the approach to writing poetry?

> **Epitaphs**
>
> Epitaphs were commemorative verses appearing on tombs or written as if intended for this appearance; they were tributes to the dead. This form seems to suit the best features of Jonson's style, with its **decorum**, clarity, proportion and classical form.

THEMES

Ben Jonson wrote this elegy after the death in 1603 of his eldest son, Benjamin, aged seven. The theme is simple and universal: a father's grief at the death of a young son.

Links

Contrasting parental attitudes

- We remember your childhood well (Carol Ann Duffy)
- My father thought it... (Simon Armitage)
- Homecoming (Simon Armitage)

Bonds between parents and children

- The Affliction of Margaret (William Wordsworth)
- Little Boy Lost/Found (William Blake)

W. B. YEATS, 1899 – The Song of the Old Mother

1 The 'Old Mother' describes how she gets up at dawn to light the fire and then works all day until night time, cleaning and cooking.

2 She describes the young in the family, asleep in their beds dreaming of trivial things. During the day they devote their time to idleness.

3 She states that she herself must work until she grows old and dies.

STRUCTURE

The structure of this poem is simple: a ten line single verse comprising of five **rhyming couplets**

DID YOU KNOW?

The 'Old Mother' could represent the mother of all Ireland, or perhaps a previous, more responsible generation.

CHECKPOINT 13

How does the **metre** contribute to the effect of this poem?

STYLE

'The Song of the Old Mother' comes from a collection of romantic poems called *The Wind among the Reeds* (1899). There is a certain song-like lilt to the rhythm of the poem, especially in the use of 'And' (lines 3, 5, 7, 8, 10) which reinforces the apparently endless toil of the woman's life. 'Musical' language is used too – Yeats had a tremendous ear for **assonance** and **alliteration**. Pick out some examples and consider the effect they are meant to have – is Yeats interested in sound for the sake of sound, or does the particular sound of the language reinforce an idea? Notice the way Yeats repeats the phrase 'seed of the fire' (line 2) in the last line but with different adjectives attached to it. Why?

THEMES

The theme is simple like the language and structure of the poem. Since Yeats was interested in Irish folk culture, he was concerned to express what he believed were the emotions of the peasant population.

Links

Maternal attitudes

- The Affliction of Margaret (William Wordsworth)

Mother at work for her children

- Mother, any distance … (Simon Armitage)

EXAMINER'S SECRET

When quoting poetry, the best technique is to 'integrate' the quote with your comment. (Like the word *integrate* in the last sentence.)

WILLIAM WORDSWORTH, 1807 – The Affliction of Margaret

❶ A mother laments the loss of her son. She asks where he could be and what has happened to him.

❷ She has not seen the boy, her only child, for seven years. To be constantly hoping to see him again and yet to be continually disappointed is hellish.

❸ He was a beautiful, well-born boy. She sent him away an

honest, innocent and confident person. Children do not realise how much power they have to upset their mothers, but this does not reduce the parent's love.

4 She refuses to continue to be self-pitying, even though she feels neglected and has shed many secret tears over the boy.

5 She asks her son not to be afraid to return to his mother, especially if he has been brought down in the world.

6 She regrets that people do not have wings like birds so that after they have wandered in the world they can return home quickly.

7 Perhaps her son is being cruelly treated in a prison. Perhaps he is in some distant land being attacked by lions. Perhaps he has drowned at sea.

8 All this talk about the dead communicating with the living is a lie. If it was true, she would have heard from the one she longs for so much.

9 Her doubts multiply. Everything upsets her. No one understands. If anybody happens to feel anything for her, it is only pity. She wishes you would come back to her, because he is her only friend in this world.

CHECK THE FILM

Pandaemonium directed by Julian Temple (USA Films, 2001) is a visually dazzling, thoughtful and intelligent film that shows how Coleridge and Wordsworth were once the equivalent of rock stars in their day.

STRUCTURE

Eleven seven-line stanzas. The poem begins with the question from which the whole piece develops – 'Where art thou...?'. Each stanza is devoted to an aspect of the woman's psychological situation, culminating in the final desolate conclusion of the last verse, 'Beyond participation lie / My troubles...' (lines 71–2).

STYLE

Although formal in design, this monologue uses the first person to create the illusion of a personal statement, an expression of profound loss. This is an 'illusion' because Wordsworth's **diction** and **syntax** are obviously that of a poet and not an actual speaking person. Notice the way 'poetic' diction is mingled with the rhythms and tone of everyday English: 'beauteous' (line 16), ' blasts of heaven' (line 44) and 'Wellborn. Well bred' (line 17), 'I dread the rustling of the grass' (line 65).

GLOSSARY

participation help/ support

? DID YOU KNOW?
'The Affliction of Margaret' is based on the case of a poor widow who lived in the town of Penrith, near the poet's home at Grasmere. Her sorrow was well known. She kept a shop, and when she saw a stranger passing by, she was in the habit of going out into the street to enquire of him after her son.

THEMES

The woman's 'affliction' is not merely the loss of her son, but not knowing what has happened to him: the unbreakable bond that a mother feels for her child.

The poem focuses on the woman's present feelings, and only fleetingly refers to the story of how she 'sent him forth' (line 17) into the world. Why do you think this is?

Links

First-person statements
- Havisham (Carol Ann Duffy)
- Kid (Simon Armitage)
- Ulysses (Alfred Tennyson)

Women's position
- The Song of the Old Mother (W. B. Yeats)

CHECKPOINT 14

Lyrical Ballads appeared in 1800. It was headed by a preface in prose that constituted Wordsworth's manifesto for a new **naturalism** in English verse. What evidence can you find in **'The Affliction of Margaret'** of Wordsworth's approach to poetry writing?

WILLIAM BLAKE, 1789 – The Little Boy Lost/Found

1 A little boy loses his way while following his father.

2 He finds himself lost in the dark night.

3 God appears to him looking like his father.

4 God leads him to his mother who is searching for him.

STRUCTURE

The shortness and simplicity of these two poems make them easy to memorise. They are obviously matched and should be read 'side by side': the turning point in the 'story' comes at the last line of '**The Little Boy Lost**', 'And away the vapour flew' (line 8).

**CHECK
THE BOOK**

As well as being a poet, throughout his life William Blake worked as a professional artist and engraver. He illustrated several editions of his own poems such as *The Book of Thel* and *Songs of Innocence*.

STYLE

Both poems have simple **diction** and **syntax**. The style is direct, almost childlike, yet weighted with a visionary effect. The vapours disappear and the boy is led by 'the wand'rng light' ('**The Little Boy Lost**' line 2) to God who replaces the father figure as a true protector of the child.

GLOSSARY
vapour mists

CHECK THE NET

William Blake on the web: **http://www. betatesters.com/ penn/blake.htm**.

THEMES

The link between parents and a child is the focus, yet, typically, it is difficult with Blake's poems to identify a straightforward theme. He makes simple things and situations carry a lot of meaning. The two poems could make up a little **allegory** of a Christian or visionary nature in which goodness and innocence are restored.

Links

Representation of childhood fears

- We Remember your Childhood Well (Carol Ann Duffy)

Parents' attitudes

- Homecoming (Simon Armitage)
- On my first Sonne (Ben Jonson)

DID YOU KNOW?

Tichborne's real name was not Charles but Chidiock!

CHARLES TICHBORNE, 1586 – Tichborne's Elegy

1 Tichborne was one of many Catholics who lost their lives during the religious persecutions in the sixteenth century.

2 In the first verse the poet lists all the good things in his life which have changed by his situation – youth, joy and hope.

3 The second verse alludes to the irony of his early death, of a life hardly lived and to his forthcoming execution.

4 The last verse confronts the inevitable, death, and implies that all people must die one day.

STRUCTURE

Each line expresses an aspect of his existence contrasted with the pain of the present. Each verse ends with same line, like a **refrain**. In structure, it is very well crafted. The 'refrain' is integrated to underline what the poet has said in each verse.

STYLE

The tone is regretful and very sad. In each line the quality named in the first half is negated in the second. For instance, in the first stanza, 'prime of youth' is contrasted with a 'frost of cares' (line 1). The contrast is between two unlike things – 'prime' (literally spring) and 'frost' (standing for winter) – making the comparison particularly stark. Another contrast, 'corn'/'tares' (line 3) – alludes to a parable found in the Christian Bible. The corn represents those who will be 'saved' and go to heaven; the 'tares' are the damned that will burn in hell.

The poet makes us feel the despair in the poem, by his use of repetition. Some of the contrasts, notably those in lines 5, 11 and 17 are not contradictory statements at all, but paradoxes related to Tichborne's early death. In fact they are true when examined closely:

> 'The day is past, and yet I saw no sun' (line 5)
> 'My thread is cut, and yet it is not spun' (line 11)
> 'My glass is full, and now my glass is run' (line 17)

Many of the contrasts are **metaphors** or instances – 'My thread is cut' (line 11), which uses the visual image of a severed thread of cotton to represent the ending of his life by death.

Even though the use of contrast is very conventional, Tichborne endows the writing with great sadness and regret through his use of

---

CHECKPOINT 15

Does the fact that this poem is in the 'true' voice of the poet make any significant difference to how you read it?

GLOSSARY

tares an injurious cornfield weed

CHECKPOINT 16

Some people might find Tichborne's elegy for himself a little mechanical, self-pitying even, in the way it is laid out in **antithetic parallelisms**. Do you agree?

imagery and through his **tone**. There is no bitterness or resentment in his voice, only a kind of weary acceptance of his fate. Naturally, because we know that this fate was real and did take place, this adds a special poignancy to the poem. You should look at how the **rhyme** and the **rhythm** in the poem help communicate this feeling of regret.

THEMES

The main idea is that, in the face of his coming execution, Tichborne feels that his life is over without his having really lived it. (He was twenty-eight.)

Links

Approaching death

- November
  (Simon Armitage)

First-person voice

- The Affliction of Margaret
  (William Wordsworth)

THOMAS HARDY, 1902 – The Man He Killed

1 A soldier reflects on the man he has killed in battle. If they had met in some other context, such as an inn, they would have sat down and drank together.

2 But lined up face to face as enemy soldiers, they shot at one another, and the speaker killed the other man as he stood in line.

3 The reason the speaker shot at him was because he was his 'foe' (line 10).

4 But probably their reasons for enlisting in the army were similar, just as casual and practical, such as being unemployed and poor.

5 Yes, the speaker concludes, war is very strange: it makes you kill someone who, if you met him in a bar, you would buy a drink, or lend 'half-a-crown' (line 20).

STRUCTURE

A simple, formal structure of five short stanzas rhyming ABAB.
The last two stanzas take up the original idea of the men being equal
and potential friends. Stanzas two and three set out the qualifying
circumstances that change everything for the men's fate: they are
soldiers in opposing armies and therefore enemies.

STYLE

Hardy imitates the speech rhythms and **diction** of an ordinary
working-class man in the process of reflecting on the tragic
circumstances that have made him kill someone very like himself.
The quotation marks within which the poem is placed remind us
that this is the direct address of a man possibly engaged in
conversation with a friend after the war.

'I shot him dead because – / Because he was my foe' (lines 9–10) and
'– just as I – / Was out of work' (lines 14–15) capture his doubtful,
faltering attempt to rationalise what happened. There are
colloquialisms such as 'Off-hand like' (line 14) which provide an
earthy **realism** along with the rough sounding **metre**

THEMES

At the end of the nineteenth century, Hardy published *Poems of
the Past and Present* (August, 1901) a few months after the death
of Queen Victoria, containing **elegies** and war **sonnets** written in
1899 on the occasion of the Boer War. This is one of those poems.
All Hardy's writing is underpinned by a strong sense of the way
men and women struggle against the fate that seems to govern their
lives and against which they are seemingly powerless. This fate, or
force, is indifferent to human suffering. It creates situations that are
full of disappointment and **irony**. Consequently, Hardy's work can
be seen as **tragic**. 'The Man He Killed' is a poem that dramatises
one of the tragic ironies that govern Hardy's universe: men are
basically the same, have the same desires and needs, yet fate in the
form of society turns them into murderous enemies.

With its spareness of **metre** and diction, its use of colloquialisms,

**DID YOU
KNOW?**

After his first wife
died, Hardy
composed some of
his greatest love
poems for her, even
though by the end
they were barely on
speaking terms. He
married his
secretary, Florence,
in 1914, a woman
thirty-nine years
younger than
himself. Apparently,
she was a very
melancholy person!

CHECKPOINT 17

How would you
read the line 'Yes;
quaint and curious
war is!' (line 17)?

and formal structure, **'The Man He Killed'** bears comparison with the contemporary poems you are studying.

Links

Sense of tragedy within the form of a personal anecdote

- November
  (Simon Armitage)

Attitude to death

- Education for Leisure
  (Carol Ann Duffy)

Intention to kill

- The Laboratory
  (Robert Browning)

WALT WHITMAN, 1856 – Patrolling Barnegat

DID YOU KNOW?

Barnegat Bay is on the coast of Ocean County, New Jersey

❶ The poem describes the sensations of a storm at midnight at Barnegat Bay.

❷ The first four lines introduce the reader to aspects of the sound of the storm – 'Shouts of demoniac laughter...' (line 3).

❸ At line 4 the three elements of this particular storm are identified: 'Waves, air, midnight, their savagest trinity lashing'.

❹ From line 5 to the final line there is a description of the scene 'Out in the shadows...' (line 5) on the shore, where 'A group of dim, weird forms...' (line 13) is patrolling the shoreline looking for signs of a shipwreck.

STRUCTURE

'Patrolling Barnegat' has the same number of lines as a **sonnet**, but with all lines **rhyming** alike. What makes it difficult to understand at first is the fact that it is written in one continuous sentence. Each line piles up more and more detail of a single 'timeless' experience. The sensation of being *within* a storm is more important to Whitman than any structuring of the experience in conventional poetic form. The use of a single, rhyming present continuous verb at the end of each line gives the sense of time slowed down, so that the reader feels disorientated, dizzy with sensory overload.

But take out the main grammatical skeleton,

- 'Out in the shadows...' (line 5)

- 'Where...' (line 6)

- 'A group of dim, weird forms...' (line 13)

- 'watching' (line 14)

and it's easier to see how Whitman has structured the poem, making the suspended appearance of the 'watching' (line 14) figures on the shoreline especially dramatic.

EXAMINER'S SECRET

Choose the questions that you have most information on and can write most about. Allocate enough time for each question.

STYLE

Like much of Whitman's poetry this poem is not simple, in spite of his claim in the preface to *Leaves of Grass* that his new style was to be 'democratic' and straightforward. At first it seems as if the long **cadenced** lines have to be taken in one breath. But note that most of the lines contain an implied pause. Line 5 for example gives first a place – 'Out in the shadows there' – followed by what is happening

DID YOU KNOW?

Walt Whitman worked as a volunteer nurse during the American Civil War.

CHECKPOINT 18

Onomatopoeia is a common feature of poetic language. Try to find some examples of it in **'Patrolling Barnegat'** and explain the effect it has.

– 'milk-white combs careering'. These slight breaks become more obvious if you read the poem aloud. They help build a tremendous **rhythm**, giving the effect of Whitman wanting to embrace the whole experience of the storm in a series of labouring breaths.

A prominent feature of **'Patrolling Barnegat'** is the dramatic use of **alliteration**. The 's' sound is taken from the key words in line 1, 'storm' and 'sea', and then repeated so that it becomes a **motif** that dominates the whole poem. Notice also how Whitman repeats certain phrases: 'milk-white combs careering' (lines 5 and 12), 'slush and sand' (lines 6 and 10). Why do you think the use of repetition is a technical feature of the poem generally?

THEMES

In 1855 Whitman issued the first of many editions of *Leaves of Grass*, a volume of a new kind of poetry considerably different to the conventional verse he had previously written. In this book Whitman praises the human body and glorifies the senses. **'Patrolling Barnegat'** uses an extraordinary range of sensory language. The poem seems to be contrasting the power ('That savage trinity', line 14) of the storm to overwhelm the senses and potentially destroy the indistinct 'warily watching' (line 14) human figures.

Links

Violent imagery
- Havisham
  (Carol Ann Duffy)

Complex sound patterns
- Inversnaid
  (Gerard Manley Hopkins)

WILLIAM SHAKESPEARE, 1609 – Sonnet 130

❶ William Shakespeare refuses to compare the woman he loves with other things as some poets do.

2 **She cannot gain in beauty as a result of elaborate comparisons.**

3 **For him she is perfect as she is.**

STRUCTURE

The poem begins with an unambiguous statement – one that would
have surprised Shakespeare's contemporaries. They expected
sonnets to contain elaborate comparisons. William Shakespeare
rejects this. Obviously the sun is brighter than her eyes (line 1),
obviously coral is a brighter shade of red than her lips (line 2).

Similarly he points out in line 3 that her breasts are flesh coloured.
They are not white like snow. How can they be?

In line 4 he asks how it is possible to compare hair with golden
threads – 'wires' – when her hair is black. He has seen roses
'damasked' (line 5) – or dappled – but he does not see anything like
this in her cheeks.

He continues his objection to artificiality and false comparisons by
saying that her breath is not always perfumed. Whilst he loves to
hear the sound of her voice he knows that music 'hath a far more
pleasing sound' (line 10).

William Shakespeare has never seen a goddess so he is not sure how
they walk but he knows that 'My mistress when she walks treads on
the ground' (line 12).

It is in the **couplet** that ends the sonnet that he states his purpose in
writing this poem. The woman he loves is a real woman, not a false
creation formed from exaggerated comparisons. He loves her for
what she is and he doesn't have to play the games of poets to prove it.

STYLE

He composes his expression of love by following the accepted formula
for a sonnet that gives it a regular pattern and **metre**. In the first
quatrain (i.e. the first four lines) he has one comparison in each line.
In the second and third quatrains he expands his descriptions to two
lines each. Then the final couplet establishes the purpose of the poem.

**CHECK
THE NET**

There are hundreds
of websites devoted
to William
Shakespeare. Some
are more reliable
than others. A very
comprehensive
website is **www.
shakespeare-
online.com**.

**DID YOU
KNOW?**

A modern reader
will see 'wires' (line
4) as a thread of
metal. To an
Elizabethan though
it would mean fine
gold threads that
were woven into
expensive hair nets.

CHECKPOINT 19

Would someone
who received a
poem like this feel
pleased with what
it said about
them?

THEMES

William Shakespeare mocks other poets who exaggerate their lover's attributes through extravagant **similes** and **metaphors**. Love does not need such things in order to be real. Women do not need to look like something else to be beautiful. He believes that he is being more honest by rejecting such comparisons that detract from her essential humanity. Line 12 which ends his objection to falsehood is the key to the whole poem.

He himself has shown honesty in line 8 where he uses the word 'reeks', an unexpected word in the context of a poem about the poet's love. This is clearly an example of poetic honesty.

Links

Other aspects of love

- The Affliction of Margaret (William Wordsworth)
- The Laboratory (Robert Browning)

Sonnet form

- Havisham (Carol Ann Duffy)
- I've made out a will (Simon Armitage)

ROBERT BROWNING, 1845 – My Last Duchess

1 The Duke of Ferrara, during a pause in dowry negotiations, takes an envoy to see his art treasures.

2 Jealous and possessive, he had his first wife murdered.

3 He shows the envoy her picture.

STRUCTURE

We are drawn immediately into the poem because it appears that the Duke is speaking to us directly. We discover later that he is speaking to the envoy of a count whose daughter he hopes to marry. He speaks with admiration of a painting of his late wife by Fra Pandolf. He admires the technique and skill (line 3). It is almost as if she is real (line 4). He invites the envoy to look at the picture closely (line 5). The artist has captured a startling likeness and remarkable facial expression (line 8).

The Duke says that whenever he allows strangers to see it they comment upon this expression, this 'spot / Of joy' (lines 14–15). As he talks though his real feelings emerge, disturbing and vicious. It was not just her husband who could bring this look to her face (line 14).

He regarded his wife as too independent, too free spirited. The expression on her face may merely have been provoked by something the artist said (lines 16–20). In fact, she was too easily pleased:

> She liked whate'er
> She looked on, and her looks went everywhere.
> (lines 23–4)

She took pleasure in everything around her at the court but this to the Duke seemed to devalue his family, for she did not seem to appreciate the honour of being married into it.

> As if she ranked
> My gift of a nine-hundred years old name
> With anybody's gift. (lines 32–4)

She did not focus her attention upon him sufficiently. He says he was unable to make clear to her the nature of her shortcomings (line 37). It was not his responsibility to correct her or teach her, 'I choose / Never to stoop' (lines 42–3). The Duke was far too proud for this. Compromise for him would be like stooping, bringing him down to what he perceived as her level.

It became clear to him that she was not treating him with the respect he deserved because of his family and name.

> Oh sir she smiled, no doubt
> Whene'er I passed her; but who passed without
> Much the same smile? (lines 43–5)

? DID YOU KNOW?

Robert Browning's wife, Elizabeth, was a much more popular poet than Robert during their time together.

CHECKPOINT 20

Do you think that the Duchess tried deliberately to upset her husband?

EXAMINER'S SECRET

Don't waste time trying to learn long quotations. Short ones are much more effective. A good quotation to learn for the examination would be 'I gave commands' (line 45).

DID YOU KNOW?

A dowry is money or property given to a husband by his new wife's family on their marriage.

CHECKPOINT 21

Why would the Duke want to give the impression of being thoughtful?

It could not go on. He tells us quite calmly but in a chilling inhuman moment 'I gave commands' (line 45).

The Duke did not have to do anything himself. Other people carried out his instructions for him. She was murdered.

She should have known instinctively what to do and it was not his place to correct her, since she did not know she was imperfect. So he replaced her with a painting that could be admired and which would never change. His wife is now as he prefers her, a picture, a possession.

He suggests to the envoy that they rejoin the rest of the group downstairs (lines 47–8). This reminds us that we are listening in to a conversation. Clearly this visit to the picture has served whatever purpose it had. He is confident that the Count, whose daughter he now wishes to marry, will offer him a suitable dowry. When he says 'his fair daughter's self…is my object' (lines 52–3) we are not inclined to believe him, particularly as it comes immediately after a reference to a financial settlement. Also the use of the word 'object' is revealing. It has a double-edged meaning, for he indeed reduced his first wife to an object. This is emphasised as they go down stairs when he refers to another piece of artwork: 'Notice Neptune …Taming a sea horse' (lines 54–5). It is a possession to be proud of, to be valued. There is no sense of horror of what he has said to the envoy as he returns to where he started, talking of craftsmanship and ownership.

STYLE

Robert Browning's great achievement in this poem is that he reveals so many possibilities by the simple technique of allowing a character to speak for himself. The reader feels as if they are being spoken to directly and so is drawn into the events as they are being described. The power of the poem – and its ability to shock – comes from its directness. It is written in **rhyming couplets** but it has the energy and flow of ordinary speech. His use of **enjambment** means that the **rhymes** rarely fall at the end of a sentence and we thus listen to what sounds like a real conversation.

He speaks in a casual conversational tone that contrasts with the horror of what he has done. To the Duke it appears absolutely acceptable. His wife was an object and when he became dissatisfied he disposed of her and decided to get a new one. He has turned her into a picture that is much easier to control. He alone can pull back the curtain in front of her.

THEMES

Lots of possibilities emerge as we piece together the story. Is he an older man trying to keep a young spirited woman in order? Perhaps she was a lively interesting woman loved by her servants as a breath of fresh air in the stifling self-important formality of the court. Perhaps life with the Duke was boring. Perhaps the Duke believed her enjoyment of life lay in flirtation; perhaps he feared she was unfaithful. Certainly he did not approve of her behaviour. It was not his responsibility to correct her. So he had her killed.

Why does he tell the envoy these things? Is it because he sees nothing wrong in the murder of his wife? Or is it a subtle warning about how he expects any new wife to behave? Like Neptune he will have to tame her and he expects to succeed. The hesitations in his speech – 'how shall I say?' (line 22) – 'I know not how' (line 32) – give him an air of bewilderment. How could these things happen? It is a puzzle to him. He presents himself throughout as a reasonable man of taste and refinement married to a young woman who lacked discrimination. The words he uses too are significant. Notice that her behaviour does not upset him or irritate him; it 'disgusts' him (line 38).

DID YOU KNOW?

Robert Browning's poem is based upon real events. Duke Alfonso II of Modena and Ferrara (1559–97) married the first of his three wives, Lucrezia de Doctors (the 'last duchess' of the poem) at Ferrara in June 1558. Lucrezia died four years later. Alfonso's second marriage in December 1565 was to Barbarian, Archduchess of Austria. She died in 1572. Alfonso's last wife (married in 1579) was Eleonora Gonzaga. She outlived Alfonso and died in 1618.

CHECKPOINT 22

Why would the Duke keep the picture behind a curtain?

Robert Browning's poem suggests all these things, and more.

Links

Jealousy and hate
- Havisham
  (Carol Ann Duffy)
- Hitcher
  (Simon Armitage)
- The Laboratory
  (Robert Browning)

Methods to create first-person persona
- Ulysses
  (Alfred Tennyson)

ROBERT BROWNING, 1845 – The Laboratory

1 A woman consults an apothecary to obtain poison in order to murder a rival.

2 She takes great pleasure in watching its preparation.

3 She is determined to enjoy her revenge.

STRUCTURE

The subtitle – Ancien Régime – places the poem in the past, in eighteenth-century France. The formal world of a royal palace is suggested. But beneath that suggestion of privilege and order there lurks hatred and revenge.

Notice how the title is an integral part of the poem, for it tells us where the scene is taking place. The speaker, a woman, ties on a mask to watch the preparation of a substance in an apothecary's laboratory. She takes pleasure in watching the procedure with its 'faint smoke curling whitely' (line 2). The last line of the first verse comes as a shock to us. It is not what a reader would normally expect from a poem. It is dramatic and arresting: 'Which is the

DID YOU KNOW?

When Robert Browning published his wife's *Sonnets* he said that they were 'the finest Sonnets written in any language since Shakespeare' poison to poison her, prithee?' (line 4). The line also tells us that it is being prepared for an identified victim.

In the second verse we begin to see why. The reason is revenge, for the speaker has been betrayed by her lover. She knows that he is with another woman and that they believe she has run off to cry in an empty church.

But she is not in a church praying to God. As she told us in the first verse, she is in 'this devil's-smithy' (line 3). She can hear them laughing at her. But she is much stronger than they think. Her reaction is not hysterical but calculated.

In verse three she watches the apothecary at work and is fascinated by what he is doing. She is in no hurry. She takes pleasure in the preparations. This is better than dancing in the king's palace.

She asks questions, taking an interest in the coloured liquids and substances. She is keen to learn and appreciates the contrast between their appearance and their effect:

> And yonder soft phial, the exquisite blue,
> Sure to taste sweetly, – is that poison too?   (lines 15–16)

It is clear in verse five that she is consumed by her need for revenge and wishes that all the contents of the Laboratory and the apothecary himself were hers, so that she could carry 'pure death' (line 19) where ever she went. The poisons are 'a wild crowd of invisible pleasures!' (line 18) and the prospect of having such power over others excites her. Her rivals may believe that she is a victim, but this will give her absolute control over life and death. Merely by using a pill or lozenge she could kill Pauline in 'just thirty minutes' (line 22) and Elise, about whose attributes she appears particularly jealous, 'should drop dead' (line 24).

She is excited now and eager in verse seven, though initially she is not happy with the colour. She wants it to be attractive so that the victim will take pleasure in taking the poison that will kill her. This

DID YOU KNOW?

Elizabeth Barrett was an invalid who spent most of her life in her room under the control of her domineering father. Robert Browning and Elizabeth conducted their courtship largely by letter.

CHECK THE NET

The Browning Pages promote all aspects of the life and work of the poet. **www. public.asu.edu**

is a further indication of her need to have power, so that she will know the true effects, even as the victim admires it.

In verse eight she says that she does not feel that this poison is sufficient. Here we found out a little more information about her rival. Perhaps it is merely jealousy that makes her say she is bigger and that she has 'masculine eyes' (line 32) but the fact remains that she wants her heart to stop beating. Last night she tried to achieve this by staring at her as the lovers whispered together, in the hope that 'she would fall / Shrivelled' (line 36). But of course this poison will be much more effective, 'Yet this does it all!' (line 36). It no longer matters that she is small. The poison will give her absolute power.

She seeks to punish her ex-lover not through his death but through the pain of watching his new love die in agony. He must have her dying face burnt forever into his memory.

There is a madness about the narrator that has slowly been revealed. In verse eleven she must remove her mask so that it will not interfere with her view of the death of her rival. She is prepared to give all her fortune for the drop that will kill.

As the poem ends she is exhilarated. She feels triumphant. Now we are given the image that would have shocked the original readers, which they would have seen as truly debased behaviour and evidence of her insanity. As she hands over her jewels as payment she tells the apothecary, who we assume to be an old man, to kiss her on her mouth.

Perhaps this is an act of revenge on her ex-lover, though more probably it indicates that she has abandoned all moral sense. She will now return to the ball where she will exact her revenge. The repetition of part of line 12, 'dance at the King's', is an indication of her excitement.

STYLE

The **rhythm** of the poem, with its positive **rhyme** scheme, is at odds with the calculating horror of the subject matter. Each verse is

> **CHECKPOINT 23**
>
> Why do you think the exclamation mark appears so frequently in the poem?

> **CHECKPOINT 24**
>
> What is the significance of the word 'ensnared' in line 30?

presented separately as a complete statement, ending in a full stop. There is no doubt, there is no moral speculation. Everything is clear and decided for this woman. It gives the poem a chilling remorselessness.

Robert Browning takes pleasurable things and turns them upside down. A dance at the palace is now an opportunity for murder. The brightly coloured attractive phials contain poison. A drink will kill. Her beautiful ball gown has dust on it that should be brushed off 'lest horror it brings' (line 47). The old apothecary should eat gold. All these details that represent the reversal of the norm, make the narrator happy and she reveals her pleasure in the anticipation of revenge. We do not hear the apothecary speak but we do not need to. Our attention is entirely focused upon the woman.

DID YOU KNOW?

When you look at this dramatic **monologue** you can imagine it acted out on the stage. Robert Browning did in fact write a number of plays, though without great success.

THEMES

The emotion behind the poem is hatred and in the grip of such hatred an unhappy woman is prepared to murder. We are drawn into her feelings because we hear her speak. It is as if we are there as she speaks to the apothecary, looking on as the poison is prepared.

As in **'My Last Duchess'** we ask questions about what is happening and this reveals possibilities. Was she in fact ever the lover of this man? Or is it a complete fantasy? Is that why they are laughing at her in verse two? Or are they actually laughing at her at all? Is she suffering from delusions and paranoia?

> ## Links
>
> **Story-telling and character**
> - The Man He Killed (Thomas Hardy)
> - My Last Duchess (Robert Browning)
>
> **Love**
> - Sonnet 130 (William Shakespeare)

ALFRED TENNYSON, 1842 – Ulysses

1 Ulysses, the legendary King of Ithaca, expresses his wish to escape from his responsibilities.

2 He wants to recapture the excitement of his past one last time before he dies.

3 He will leave his throne to his son and set sail into the sunset.

STRUCTURE

The first verse of five lines reveals in one sentence the extent of Ulysses' unhappiness. He is no longer interested in the role he has to play. He is bored, his home has no warmth and he seems to have little affection for his wife. He regards the people he rules as 'a savage race' (line 4) who concern themselves with petty disputes and merely with day-to-day survival.

If the first verse tells us what he has got in Ithaca, then the second verse outlines what he would like to have in its place. His own desires are different from those of his people. Ulysses wants to recapture the past, to recapture the excitement of his youth. This part of his life brought him the extremes of emotion, pleasure and pain (lines 7–9). He became famous 'For always roaming with a hungry heart' (line 12). He was inquisitive, an explorer and a great

DID YOU KNOW?

Tennyson is the only poet ever to be ennobled on the basis of his skill as a writer.

DID YOU KNOW?

Ithaca, the island kingdom of Ulysses, is now thought to have been what we call Cephalonia.

warrior who fought at Troy. These experiences defined his life and
everything else since then has clearly been an anticlimax. He would
like to recapture that time, for there is still much that he has not
seen. There is an:

> ...untravelled world, whose margin fades
> For ever and for ever when I move.   (lines 20–21)

He believes that he must make the most of the time he has left. He
does not want to 'rust unburnished, not to shine in use' (line 23).
This is not the time to accept restrictions. In fact Ulysses says that
to stay in one place is to believe that all there is to life is breathing
(line 24). He knows that he has little left of his own life but that
means that each hour is precious, 'saved / From that eternal silence'
(lines 26-7). Although he is old – a 'gray spirit' (line 30) – he wants
to learn new things:

> To follow knowledge like a sinking star,
> Beyond the utmost bound of human thought.   (lines 31–2)

Ulysses begins the third verse by telling us that he has decided to
pass on the responsibility for government to his son Telemachus.
He wants the task and has the patience to make a good ruler who
will help his subjects and 'through soft degrees / Subdue them to the
useful and the good' (lines 37–8). He does not share his father's
frustration and restlessness but is 'centred in the sphere / Of
common duties' (lines 39–40). Ulysses accepts that he himself has
no interest in day to day responsibility: 'He works his work, I mine'
(line 43).

The final verse is addressed to his crew, to 'My mariners' (line 45).
They have spent much time together and have experienced many
things. They may be old but something noble and significant may
still be achieved before 'Death closes all' (line 51). They can perhaps
relive their youth when they were 'men that strove with gods'
(line 53).

When Ulysses now talks about the end of the day, he is of course
talking about the end of his life: ''Tis not too late to seek a newer

DID YOU KNOW?

Troy was an ancient
city, probably in
present day Turkey
which an army of
Greeks besieged for
ten years before it
fell when the
defenders were
tricked by the
wooden horse.
These stories,
loosely based upon
historical events,
formed the basis of
many influential
legends such as the
Iliad and the
Odyssey.

CHECKPOINT 25

What does
'eternal silence'
mean in line 27?

CHECKPOINT 26

What is Ulysses'
opinion of his
subjects in Ithaca?

world' (line 57). He wants to explore the furthest extremes of the
world before it is too late and his purpose is:

> To sail beyond the sunset, and the baths
> Of all the western stars, until I die.   (lines 60–61)

They may indeed reach the 'Happy Isles' (line 63) where great
heroes like 'Achilles' (line 64) were taken after their deaths. Though
they are not as strong as they were, they have a determination to
explore and to test themselves one last time.

> **? DID YOU KNOW?**
>
> Achilles was a great warrior and hero of Homer's *Iliad* who was killed when he was shot in the heel by an arrow fired by Paris at the siege of Troy.

STYLE

The poem is written as **blank verse** which gives a natural quality to
Ulysses' speech and is divided into four verses with distinct themes.
The **rhythm** of the poem, created by the uses of **enjambment** and
caesuras is slow and almost hypnotic as befits an old man setting
out on one last adventure and disappearing from the everyday
world.

> **? DID YOU KNOW?**
>
> Near the end of his life Tennyson made a recording of himself on wax cylinders reciting his work. So we can still hear his voice today.

THEMES

The poem is an example of how the title can be an integral part of
the work. If we know who Ulysses was then we can fill in more of
the background. Once we do this, a slightly different picture of the
man may emerge.

In the original Greek legends, Ulysses was called Odysseus and the famous poem by Homer, the *Odyssey*, is about his ten-year journey home after the end of the Trojan War. He has many adventures where he is saved by his intelligence and resourcefulness. When he finally arrives home he finds that his wife Penelope has waited for him, confident that he will return.

Some people might now see Ulysses as a man who is attempting to escape from his responsibilities and who repays his wife for her loyalty by returning to a self-indulgent lifestyle of travel and adventure. Do his mariners really want to leave their homes once more? Will they really share his enthusiasm?

If we pursue this interpretation, then Ulysses' stately and measured language becomes rather pompous. This of course is one of the defining qualities of the **dramatic monologue,** that it can support different interpretations as values in society change over time. A Victorian reader may not have accepted this version but a reader hearing Ulysses speak today may well interpret his words in a critical way.

All the excitement that made Ulysses famous happened when he was younger. Now he is living in the shadow of that fame. Nothing that has happened since has ever rivalled the pleasure of those days. He speaks of his desire to recapture his youth before it is too late. He wishes to leave responsibility, to escape the tedium of his life and turn back the clock. He does not want to fulfil his obligations to his wife, his son or his subjects. But he will have to face up to the reality of aging and of death. He will seek and explore before he does indeed meet up with Achilles in death.

 DID YOU KNOW?

Tennyson was tall and very strong. He once carried a pony round the table during dinner!

Links

Attitude to death

- November (Simon Armitage)
- Tichborne's Elegy (Charles Tichborne)

Re-creation of mythological character

- Salome (Carol Ann Duffy)

OLIVER GOLDSMITH, 1770 – The Village Schoolmaster

1 This is an extract from a much longer poem called 'The Deserted Village'.

2 Oliver Goldsmith remembers the village schoolmaster and the effect and influence he had upon his pupils and the community as a whole.

3 A once-thriving village is now deserted as the inhabitants have moved away.

4 The poet thinks back to a time when it was busy and full of life.

DID YOU KNOW?

Although Goldsmith was socially very clumsy and people often laughed at him, the artist Joshua Reynolds said of him, 'Wherever he was there was no yawning'

STRUCTURE

As he walks round the village, Oliver Goldsmith points out the old village school. It was a noisy place but the schoolmaster was 'skilled to rule' (line 3) and was in complete control. Truants knew that they would be dealt with firmly, for he was very strict (line 5). They would try to win favour by laughing loudly at his jokes 'with counterfeited glee' (line 9). He knew lots of jokes and the implication is that he expected his pupils to laugh at them.

Certainly his moods were a vital part of the classroom, affecting everyone else and were thus carefully observed:

> Full well the busy whisper, circling round
> Conveyed the dismal tidings when he frowned; (lines 11–12)

The repetition of the words 'Full well' in lines 9 and 11 links the light hearted moments in the classroom with these more tense occasions.

Oliver Goldsmith, though, excuses him. He was kind and, if he appeared rather too strict, it was only because he believed in the importance of learning (lines 13–14). He was much respected by the small community in which he lived. To them his knowledge seemed incredible, for he had skills that they did not possess in writing and mathematics (lines 15–16). He could calculate 'terms' (line 17) and anticipate the seasons and festivals, a skill that to simple villagers without calendars appeared remarkable. In fact they really believed he was so clever that he could even calculate the volume of barrels (line 18). They were indeed in awe of his vocabulary and his knowledge:

> And still they gazed, and still the wonder grew
> That one small head could carry all he knew. (lines 23–4)

STYLE

Oliver Goldsmith's **couplets** reflect the status the schoolmaster had. They have positive **rhymes,** each couplet ending in a definitive piece of punctuation that gives the rhymes additional emphasis. The first twelve lines deal with the schoolmaster as he is in school. The second twelve deal with his importance to the whole village.

THEMES

The poem displays the complete respect that the villagers had for the schoolmaster who was a giant in their small community. However, Goldsmith's implied attitude is coloured by a very delicate **irony.** Can you detect where a more critical attitude is implied in the poem?

Oliver Goldsmith gives a picture of the villagers themselves and their simple lives. Isolated villages relied upon individuals who could read, who could predict festivals, even days of the week, and solve disputes. A little knowledge would make them very important people in the village.

Links

Attitude of author to subject
- The Affliction of Margaret (William Wordsworth)
- My Last Duchess (Robert Browning)

Poetic form
- Kid (Simon Armitage)
- The Laboratory (Robert Browning)

CHECKPOINT 27

What impressed the villagers about the schoolmaster's vocabulary?

 DID YOU KNOW?

Oliver Goldsmith spent a year touring Europe in 1755. He supported himself by playing the flute.

ALFRED TENNYSON, 1851 – The Eagle

1 Alfred Tennyson describes an eagle that looks down upon the world.

2 He tries to capture the presence and the power of the eagle in two short verses.

? DID YOU KNOW?

Alfred Tennyson is usually referred to as Alfred, Lord Tennyson after he was made a baron in 1884.

www. CHECK THE NET

The Victorian Web has a great deal of very useful information on the Victorian age, including pages on Gerard Manley Hopkins, Alfred Tennyson and Robert Browning:
www.65.107.211. 206/Victorian.

STRUCTURE

The bird 'clasps the crag' (line 1) as if he owns it. He stands there in splendid isolation. He is close to the sun, much closer than man can ever be, surrounded by the blue of the sky (line 3). This is his world, not the world of man.

The eagle can look down upon the sea below him. It is so far beneath him that it seems 'wrinkled' and it 'crawls' (line 4), a word that strips the ocean of its majesty. Real power lies with the eagle who, when he chooses, can fall from the 'mountain walls' (line 5) where he sits 'like a thunderbolt' (line 6). This **simile** emphasises the huge power that the bird possesses.

STYLE

The first line is dominated by hard 'c' sounds – 'clasps', 'crags' and 'crooked'. These words immediately establish the nature of the bird as fierce, domineering and in control.

Tennyson here is particularly interested in capturing the eagle's power and its haughty superiority perched in the mountains.

THEMES

There is no doubt about the bird's gender. It is reinforced in every line except line two. Perhaps something of the Victorian male's sense of his own power and superiority is reflected by this depiction.

Yet in this poem, animals inhabit a different world which man cannot access. We can watch the eagle in the sky but we can never experience its world.

Links

Use of powerful imagery
- Patrolling Barnegat
  (Walt Whitman)

Rhyming structure
- Kid
  (Simon Armitage)

CHECKPOINT 29

Which part of the eagle does Tennyson **not** refer to directly in the first line but which is implied?

GERARD MANLEY HOPKINS, 1881 – Inversnaid

❶ Gerard Manley Hopkins describes the experience of watching a mountain stream turn into a waterfall.

STRUCTURE

'Inversnaid' has a simple inspiration. What Gerard Manley Hopkins attempts is to use words to describe the complete experience of watching the stream and a waterfall. By compressing words together he is able to give a much more intense impression.

 CHECK THE NET

This Gerard Manley Hopkins website has lots of material about the poet:
www. creighton. edu/~dcallon/ Hopkins.

DID YOU KNOW?

Inversnaid is on the north-eastern shore of Loch Lomond in the west of Scotland.

CHECKPOINT 30

The waterfall that Gerard Manley Hopkins writes about is called The Mare's Tail. How do you think this could have influenced the making of poem?

DID YOU KNOW?

'Sprung Rhythm' was an attempt by Gerard Manley Hopkins to introduce a new rhythm to the structure of poetry, which he hoped would bring it closer to common speech.

We can see this immediately in the first two lines. The stream ('burn') is 'horseback brown'. This suggests the colour of the water and also the speed of its movement. It roars down, the word 'rollrock' (line 2) describing its power. It creates foam (line 3) that looks like wool on the water.

This foam is caught by a 'windpuff' (line 5) as the water falls into a pool and circles around. The pool where it enters is so dark that it appears to have the power to wipe away all emotion (line 8). This darkness could be a symbol of despair, perhaps a symbol of life disappearing. But the water has such force that it drowns out such human feelings.

Gerard Manley Hopkins then moves on in verse three to describe the land on either side of the stream. It is wild untended moorland with 'Wiry heathpacks' (line 11). Such wild places, untouched by mankind, should be preserved because they speak of the power of the natural world:

> What would the world be, once bereft
> Of wet and of wildness? Let them be left, (lines 13–14)

STYLE

This is a very musical poem, held together by its regular **rhyme** scheme and by the use of **consonants**. This is called **assonance**. In the first verse, for example, the dominant sounds are '*b*', '*r*' and '*f*'. As verse two moves into verse three the sound turns to '*d*' and in the final verse the '*w*' sound dominates.

This musicality gives the poem its power and **rhythm**. It flows, with the hard sounds suggesting the way the water rushes and splashes and slaps on the rocks. These are things associated with a fast-moving stream. Gerard Manley Hopkins is attempting to make you feel as if you are there watching the waterfall drop down into a pool. He compresses its energy into carefully chosen words. The dark water is like a powerful horse rocking at speed down a road. The water has the power to move rocks. All this is suggested in the first ten words of the poem.

In the second verse there is a clear progression in emotions. We start with 'frowning' (line 7) which leads to 'Despair' (line 8) which leads perhaps to suicide – 'drowning' (line 8) – in the hypnotic circling of the water. These words reflect Gerard Manley Hopkins' feelings at this time. However the power of the water wipes away all such human uncertainty.

The plea in the last verse, that such places should remain untouched, is emphasised by the repetition of key words.

THEMES

Gerard Manley Hopkins' relationship with nature marks this out as an important poem. He displays unquestioning admiration for nature and attempts to create a complete picture of a natural phenomenon.

In 'Inversnaid' there is no human influence. That is part of its attraction to the poet. Here he can escape from the pressures and tensions of his life and lose himself in the power of nature.

Links

Nature

- Patrolling Barnegat
  (Walt Whitman)
- The Eagle
  (Alfred Tennyson)
- Sonnet
  (John Clare)

Verbal patterning

- Havisham
  (Carol Ann Duffy)
- Kid
  (Simon Armitage)

> **? DID YOU KNOW?**
> The poem was written on 28 September 1881.

> **? DID YOU KNOW?**
> After a break from writing poetry (see **Setting and background**), Gerard Manley Hopkins was inspired to start writing poetry again by the sinking of a ship called *The Deutschland* at the mouth of the river Thames in 1875, in which five nuns were drowned. He offered the poem to the Jesuit journal *The Month* but the editor said that he dared not publish it!

JOHN CLARE, 1841 – Sonnet

1 John Clare reveals his admiration for nature.

2 He identifies the things that he likes to see.

STRUCTURE

John Clare tells us about the things in nature that he enjoys. It is above all else a personal statement of an uncomplicated relationship with nature. He tells us of the things he sees that give him pleasure.

He enjoys the summer brightness and the white clouds in the sky, the wild flowers, the water lilies. He describes an idyllic scene, with rustling reeds and nesting moorhens. The willow hanging over the 'clear deep lake' (line 10) has a perfect shape.

John Clare provides us with a vivid description. It is not, though, a static one. It has in it a sense of movement as if the poem is powered by the summer breeze. The white clouds are 'sailing to the north' (line 2), the moorhen's nest is 'floating' (line 8), the 'flower head swings' (line 11). The insects are flying on 'happy wings' (line 12) and the beetles seem to be playing in the 'clear lake' (line 14). Nature is at ease with itself, happy and untroubled. The water is pure and there is no intrusion from human beings.

STYLE

The **sonnet** has a simple pattern, the traditional fourteen lines, here presented as seven **couplets**. It has a regularity and a shape. The lack of punctuation ensures that the poem maintains a rhythm that places emphasis upon the rhymed words. The words 'I love' are repeated three times along with 'I like'. This helps to tie the piece together and states clearly the feelings that have inspired John Clare to write. Such simplicity is a feature of his work and makes his poetry very accessible.

THEMES

The poem has an innocence at its heart. Nature is attractive and balanced with no need of humankind. It is something that exists to make the poet feel better. He enjoys looking at it as if it were a painting. In this way it provides an important contrast with the work of other poets in this selection.

Gerard Manley Hopkins tries to give us the complete experience of a wild and untamed landscape. John Clare, however, describes what

---

? DID YOU KNOW?

At the time this poem was written Clare's mental instability was becoming established; perhaps we can see in it a yearning for healing, peace and simplicity.

CHECKPOINT 31

What words are used at the start of some of the lines that indicate that this poem is a very personal picture?

he sees in an uncomplicated way. There is clearly a difference in the scenes that are presented, with the wilderness of Inversnaid emphasised by the power of the water that contrasts with the gentle pastoral scene and the tranquil clear lake that Clare can see. In both cases, though, nature persists without the need for mankind.

When we realise that this poem was written when his mental instability was becoming established, perhaps we can then see in it a yearning for healing peace and simplicity.

Links

Nature
- Patrolling Barnegat (Walt Whitman)
- The Eagle (Alfred Tennyson)
- Inversnaid (Gerard Manley Hopkins)

Now take a break!

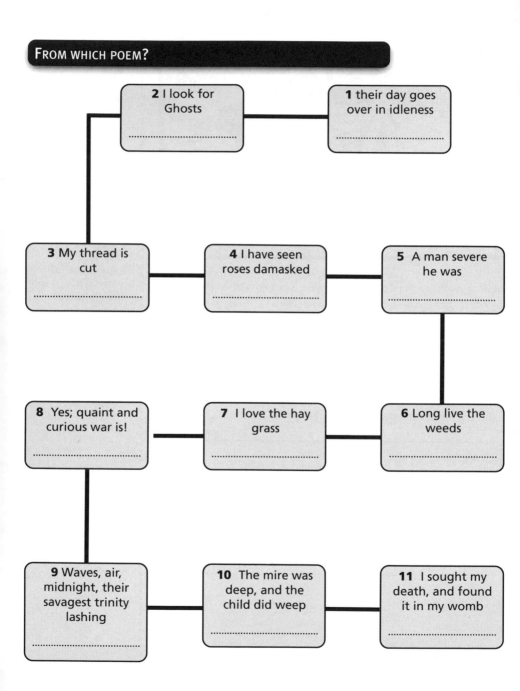

FROM WHICH POEM?

2 I look for Ghosts

....

1 their day goes over in idleness

....

3 My thread is cut

....

4 I have seen roses damasked

....

5 A man severe he was

....

8 Yes; quaint and curious war is!

....

7 I love the hay grass

....

6 Long live the weeds

....

9 Waves, air, midnight, their savagest trinity lashing

....

10 The mire was deep, and the child did weep

....

11 I sought my death, and found it in my womb

....

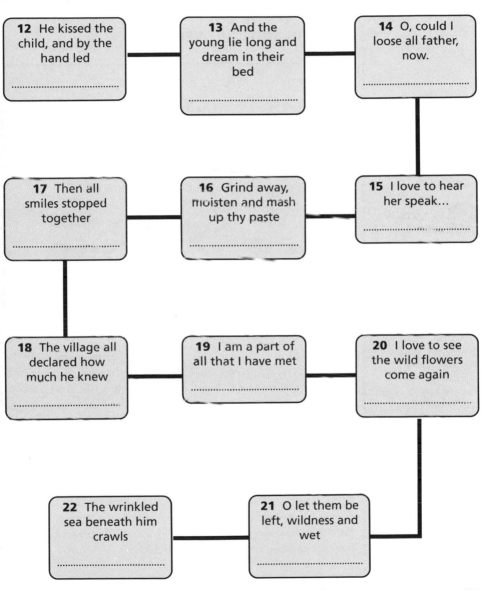

12 He kissed the child, and by the hand led

13 And the young lie long and dream in their bed

14 O, could I loose all father, now.

17 Then all smiles stopped together

16 Grind away, moisten and mash up thy paste

15 I love to hear her speak...

18 The village all declared how much he knew

19 I am a part of all that I have met

20 I love to see the wild flowers come again

22 The wrinkled sea beneath him crawls

21 O let them be left, wildness and wet

Check your answers on p. 130.

PART THREE

COMMENTARY

PARENTS AND CHILDREN

Key poems

Carol Ann Duffy	Before You Were Mine
Carol Ann Duffy	We Remember Your Childhood Well
Simon Armitage	Mother, any distance
Simon Armitage	My father thought it bloody queer
Simon Armitage	Homecoming
Simon Armitage	Kid
Ben Jonson	On my first Sonne
W. B. Yeats	The Song of the Old Mother
William Wordsworth	The Affliction of Margaret
William Blake	Little Boy Lost/Found

EXAMINER'S SECRET

It is quite extraordinary how many candidates don't actually answer the question. Be sure you know what it is you have to do before you start! You will find it helpful to keep focussed by regularly mentioning the question in your answer.

IDEAS, ATTITUDES AND FEELINGS

There are many different ideas, attitudes and feelings reflected in the poems that feature parents and children. **'Mother any distance'** and **'Before You Were Mine'** show both poets writing about an attachment to their mothers, but from male and female perspectives. Armitage's narrator is in the process of trying to break free from an umbilical – and if you are fond of **symbolism**, the tape is an obvious one for this! – attachment to his mother: he wants to 'fly'; she keeps him steady – 'Anchor. Kite' (line 8).

Duffy's poem is almost a love poem, in the sense that Duffy longs to possess her mother as she was before Carol Ann was born – 'That glamorous love lasts' (line 19). The voice in this poem appears to be far more personal and sincere than Armitage's.

Breaking free of a powerful childhood influence is the theme of **'Kid'**. Reread the poem as the speech of a step-son who has grown up and is looking back and you will see how persuasively Armitage has fitted a popular modern myth to a common domestic situation. **'Homecoming'** shows tensions between parents and children, where the mother's high standards of behaviour ('the very model of a model of a mother', line 8) are gently parodied.

'My father thought it bloody queer' and **'On my first Sonne'** show aspects of father-son relationships in vastly different contexts. The father in the Armitage poem expresses his concern and love for his adolescent son in humorously critical terms, an attitude that is taken up in the mature narrator's account of events – 'And even then I hadn't had the nerve' (line 6). By the end of the poem, the son as an adult feels both a sense of loss, and of what he has inherited, when he finds himself speaking in his father's voice, 'cried from way back in the spiral of the ear' (line 14).

Another more conventional kind of loss is expressed in Jonson's poem. He believes that his young son's death has been caused by his own sin: 'My sinne was too much hope of thee, lov'd boy' (line 2). Yet he thinks that he should not be lamenting because his much-loved son is now beyond earthly pain – 'To have so soone scap'd worlds, and fleshes rage' (line 7).

Childhood fears are the subject of Duffy's **'We Remember Your Childhood Well'** and Blake's **'Little Boy Lost / Found'**. In the former, the attitude of the speaker is one of total denial, but we sense another story that only the silent listener could provide. We have to infer what might have happened from the partial information given by the speaker. The whole poem is pervaded by a sense of threat, as if the real story exists in the silences between the abrupt sentences. The Blake poems come from his *Songs of Innocence*. Here the depiction of childhood fears is more universal than in Duffy: the 'little boy' loses his father in the first poem and is restored to his mother by God in the second. All the poems in *Songs of Innocence* have happy endings similar to this.

'The Affliction of Margaret' by Wordsworth and **'The Song of the Old Mother'** by W. B. Yeats are poems about the feelings of mothers. The 'old mother' in the Yeats poem is oppressed by the

EXAMINER'S SECRET

In your answers, say what you have to say, then finish. Don't fill up pages and pages with the repetition of one or two points supported by large chunks of quotation. A good answer is carefully structured and contains a developed commentary with integrated short quotations.

CHECK THE BOOK

If you are interested in writing poems yourself, an excellent guide has been written by Simon Armitage's old tutor, Peter Sansom: *Writing Poems* (Bloodaxe Poetry Handbooks: 2).

repetitive chores she must perform while the young people 'lie long and dream in their bed' (line 5). She is typical of many old women who exist in poor parts of the world, and whose lives are dominated by endless practical responsibilities. The title of Wordsworth's poem indicates the psychological situation of Margaret: she has lost contact with her son who has left home, although we are not given the precise reasons why. Perhaps Margaret lost her son in painful circumstances; perhaps she is a single mother (a situation carrying considerable social stigma in those days); whatever the 'story', she feels totally isolated and grief stricken – 'I have no other earthly friend' (line 77).

METHODS

Imagery

In poetry, ideas, attitudes and feelings are most likely to be represented by **imagery**. In the simplest sense, an image is some kind of word-picture of some visible scene or object. More commonly, imagery refers to the **figurative language** in a piece of literature, poetry or prose. The two key forms of imagery are **metaphor** and **simile**. They always involve a comparison between object and idea. When Simon Armitage writes, in **'Mother, any distance'**, 'the acres of the walls, the prairies of the floors' (line 4) he is using metaphors that imply a sense of space and freedom, the two things which a young man trying to be independent needs. In **'Before You Were Mine'** by Carol Ann Duffy, the **simile** 'I see you, clear as scent' (line 14) yokes together in **paradoxical** form the senses of sight and smell as powerful evocations of the imagined past.

In **'Kid'** the changed attitude of the 'kid' is conveyed in images of clothing – the cute and childish 'off-the-shoulder / Sherwood-Forest-green and scarlet number' (lines 15–16) has been exchanged for the hard realism of 'jeans and crew-neck jumper' (line 17).

'My father thought it bloody queer' and **'On my first Sonne'** contain metaphors that summarise key ideas or emotions of fathers and sons. The wound left by the botched ear piercing in the Armitage poem 'wept' (line 11) after a 'sleeper' (line 10) had been inserted. The painful emotions from this episode re-awaken again when the twenty-nine-year-old speaker hears his 'own voice breaking like a tear' (line 13). In **'On my first Sonne'** Jonson uses the extended metaphor of comparing his son's life to a loan that he has had to repay. This comes from a time when it was believed that everyone belonged to God and were only permitted to live in this world by Him.

Duffy's **'We Remember Your Childhood Well'** and Blake's **'Little Boy Lost / Found'** use contrasting imagery of childhood fears. In Duffy's poem, there is a very real sense of a hellish loss of innocence in the image 'a *Film Fun* / laughing itself to death in the coal fire' (lines 5–6), an idea that is taken up in the last stanza: '...nobody left the skidmarks of sin / on your soul and laid you wide open for Hell' (lines 16 17). Even though Blake's imagery is more simple – and even naive – he does communicate a powerful feeling of lonely terror in the line 'The mire was deep, and the child did weep' (line 7). Such simplicity gives the idea and the emotion a universal appeal. It goes beyond conventional metaphor and becomes **symbolic**.

'The Affliction of Margaret' by William Wordsworth and **'The Song of the Old Mother'** by W. B. Yeats use similar methods of image-making to communicate the feelings and situations of the two mothers.

Wordsworth may have wanted to avoid the high-flown language of the conventional poetry of his day, yet to many readers his poems have become almost the definition of poetry. (After all, he *is* responsible for the most famous simile in all poetry: 'I wandered lonely as a cloud'). In **'The Affliction of Margaret'** he lets the speaker express her psychological state in lines like 'My apprehensions come in crowds; / I dread the rustling of the grass; / The very shadows of the clouds' (lines 64–6). These uses of ordinary everyday imagery give the woman's feelings a greater authenticity.

In **'The Song of the Old Mother'** the image of the fire, which she has had to start up in the morning and keep going all day, returns again in the last line to reinforce the comparison between it and the old woman's life: 'And the seed of the fire gets feeble and cold' (line 10). As in Wordsworth, the ordinary everyday image has a close connection with the circumstances of the woman's life.

EXAMINER'S SECRET
Know the poems in detail because markers like to read very specific and *detailed* answers.

Diction

The kind of vocabulary that a poet chooses to use reveals a lot about his or her attitude to poetry and how as an art form it can communicate ideas and feelings. The **diction** of a work may be abstract or concrete, simple or elaborate, **colloquial** or formal, literal or full of **figurative language**

'Before You Were Mine', 'Mother, any distance', 'My father thought it bloody queer' and 'Kid' all use colloquial, informal diction. **'Before You Were Mine'** is written to sound as if the poet was actually talking to her mother – '…and whose small bites on your neck, sweetheart?' (line 15). Simon Armitage's **'Mother, any distance'** and **'My father thought it bloody queer'** also address directly his mother and his father, but the effect seems to be less personal than in Duffy. Colloquial diction in the Armitage poems occurs within a more formal arrangement of lines: 'two floors below your fingertips still pinch / the last one-hundredth of an inch' (**'Mother, any distance'**, lines 12–13). Try to find some examples of colloquial diction within a formal context in **'Kid'**. You will see that this creates a kind of distancing effect between the reader and the poem.

'On my first Sonne' contains diction that is simple and direct. Jonson uses figurative language sparingly, a fact that reflects his intellectual and emotional honesty – 'O, could I loose all father, now' (line 5).

Rhyme

When two words sound similar you have a **rhyme**. Most people believe this is what makes a poem; indeed the word has often been used as a **synonym** for poetry. When writing about the structure of poetry be sure you do *not* go to a lot of trouble to point out all the words that rhyme and when and how – the examiner won't be interested!

Rhyme, like **assonance**, **alliteration** and **metre**, helps provide the *musical* pleasures of poetry. Its relationship to meaning is far more indirect than **metaphors** or **similes**. In **'We Remember Your Childhood Well'** Carol Ann Duffy does not have a regular rhyme

DID YOU KNOW?

There are no words that rhyme with the word 'purple', Can you think of any other non-rhyming words?

scheme, but she uses rhymes throughout the poem. For example there are **half-rhymes** – 'tune' and 'boom' in the fourth stanza – used to underline a connection between two words. And in the final stanza **internal rhymes** are used like 'Hell' and 'well' which create a sinister, bell-like sound to finish off the poem.

In '**Little Boy Lost/Found**', '**The Affliction of Margaret**' and '**The Song of the Old Mother**', the rhyming schemes are regular. Wordsworth's poem employs one of the most basic rhyme schemes – *ababccc* – and is written with a simple **metre**. This simplicity does not stop Wordsworth being somewhat 'wordy' though. Unlike Jonson, who prided himself on the economy and precision of his rhyming technique, Wordsworth often elaborates an idea beyond what is necessary. '**The Song of the Old Mother**' has an even simpler scheme, **rhyming couplets** throughout. The metre is mostly **anapaestic** (two short stresses followed by a long), providing something of a lilting rhythm to the poem.

Assonance

Assonance is the vowel equivalent of **alliteration**, when two words of the stressed vowel sound the same, or nearly the same, e.g. the 'ee' sounds (in '**Mother, any distance**') – 'then l<u>ea</u>ving / up the stairs, the line still f<u>ee</u>ding out, unr<u>ee</u>ling / years b<u>e</u>tw<u>ee</u>n us' (lines 6–8). The drawn out sound reflects the tape being pulled out to its maximum length, and perhaps a sense of strain. Duffy uses assonance to similar effect in the line 'I wanted the b<u>o</u>ld girl winking in P<u>o</u>rt<u>o</u>bell<u>o</u>' ('**Before You Were Mine**', line 18) the 'o' sounds expressing the yearning of the daughter's emotions.

Generally, assonance is used to subtly bind the chosen words into a pattern of sound, so you should look for the repetition of vowel sounds across several lines and not just in one line. Most importantly, your comments should relate to your understanding of the way this effect relates to the meaning of a poem.

Alliteration

Alliteration is very common in both poetry and prose and is one of the most easily identifiable figures of speech. It is used to emphasise

---

DID YOU KNOW?
Spelling is not always related to pronunciation and it is important to remember this. Look at the pronunciation of the letters 'ough' in this example, where one letter is added each time:

- Tough
- Trough
- Through
- Thorough

a series of words by repeating the same consonant, e.g. 'And the young lie long and dream in their bed' (**'The Song of the Old Mother'**, line 5). Here the pairs of sounds ('l's and 'd's) appear in the important words, with 'long' and 'dream' stressed.

'The Affliction of Margaret' contains alliterating 's' sounds – 'wildest scream' etc – that culminate in the last stanza with 'Then come to me, my Son, or send / Some tidings that my woes may end' (lines 75–6) which reflect the painful emotions of the woman.

Use of first-person persona

EXAMINER'S SECRET

It is all right to say that a poem *seems* autobiographical, but you should talk about the 'voice' of the poem or the 'narrator', 'speaker', or poetic persona rather that the poet him/herself.

There are two kinds of **first-person persona** that you need to consider. The first is when the narrative is written in the voice of a dramatised persona, for example Margaret in **'The Affliction of Margaret'** or the Duke in **'My Last Duchess'**. This persona can be anonymous.

The other kind of first-person persona is when the author writes directly in the first-person *as if* he or she were writing autobiographically, for example Simon Armitage in **'November'** or **'Mother, any distance'**. What you must remember is that in both cases the author has *constructed* the narrator, so that it doesn't follow in either that the speaker can be equated with the actual author, or that the events described actually happened.

When you read a poem that is written in the voice of a dramatised narrator, it is important to remember that most of the time you will be reading *between the lines*, i.e. inferring the **subtext** of the narrative. For example, in Duffy's **'We Remember Your Childhood Well'** the unnamed narrator, who is clearly some kind of parent figure, says:

> Nobody sent you away. That was an extra holiday, with people you seemed to like. They were firm, there was nothing to fear. There was none but yourself to blame if it ended in tears.
>
> (lines 13–15)

All we are given is the speaker's version of the events, yet the language Duffy has chosen, and the way it is arranged, makes us uneasy about its truth. It's not only too emphatic, but uses words and phrases that alert us to the possible experience of the silent listener – 'people / you seemed to like', 'firm', 'fear', 'it ended in tears'

In comparison, the narrator of **'My father thought it bloody queer'** is of course Simon Armitage who, apparently, is a real person. But what if you discovered that the events depicted in it never took place? Would it make any difference to the way you read the poem? Perhaps if it does, it should not. What gives the poem its 'truth' is the detail that it contains, so that, while you are reading it, the poem is, in a sense, believable and therefore 'true'. Take the phrase 'half hidden by a mop of hair' (line 3). From this we can derive both the father's attitude, which is that a 'ring of silver' (line 2) is effeminate ('bloody queer', line 1), and the teenage Simon's rather awkward and uncertain manner. It is all there in one small, brilliant detail.

You might like to compare these two modern poems with a couple from the Pre-1914 Poetry Bank. **'On my first Sonne'** and **'The Song of the Old Mother'** would be appropriate because both first-person narrators function in a similar way to the two poems by Armitage and Duffy.

Jonson and Yeats use more formal structures and **diction** than the modern poets and this might affect the way you read them. You might be less prepared to become involved in what they are about because they seem more remote from your experience than the more **colloquial** modern poets. However, both writers seem to have an equally accessible and direct way of writing. In Jonson's case this could be related to the fact that the poem is about a real event. In this context, Jonson's 'I' expresses ideas and attitudes that were commonplace for his time. In the seventeenth century, the mortality rate was high, especially among young children, and Jonson probably sincerely believed that his dead son was in a better place than this world and consequently should be genuinely envied (line 6).

> **CHECKPOINT 32**
>
> How do you think the persona of the old mother in the Yeats poem compares to the one in **'We Remember Your Childhood Well'**?

LOVE AND HATE

> ### Key poems
>
> | Carol Ann Duffy | **Havisham** |
> | Carol Ann Duffy | **Anne Hathaway** |
> | Simon Armitage | **Homecoming** |
> | William Shakespeare | **Sonnet 130** |
> | Robert Browning | **My Last Duchess** |
> | Robert Browning | **The Laboratory** |
> | John Clare | **Sonnet** |

DID YOU KNOW?

'How do I love thee? Let me count the ways' is a famous line from one of Elizabeth Barrett's poems about Robert Browning. If you look at the poem, she identifies eleven ways that she loves him.

IDEAS, ATTITUDES AND FEELINGS

Several of these poems contain vivid portrayals of characters who are in the grip of extreme human emotions. You can find the bitterness of frustrated desire in 'Havisham', murderous jealousy in 'The Laboratory', cold pride in 'My Last Duchess', romantic love in 'Sonnet 130', and romantic memories of love in 'Anne Hathaway'. Simon Armitage's 'Homecoming', by contrast, seems to express a quieter, implicit tenderness.

'Sonnet 130' and 'Anne Hathaway' reflect their author's deep concern for language and the way it links to erotic human emotions. In Shakespeare's **sonnet** the poet praises his mistress by rejecting the familiar comparisons of love poetry, which he regards as 'false' (line 14). He lists all the things one might expect to find in a conventional love poem – 'the sun' (line 1), 'Coral' (line 2), 'snow' (line 3), 'roses' (line 5), 'perfumes' (line 7), 'music' (line 10), 'a goddess' (line 11) – and dismisses them as idealistic, concluding that his mistress is still 'as rare / as any she belied with false compare' (lines 13–14). It is appropriate that Duffy should make Shakespeare's widow, Anne Hathaway, write in the sonnet form because that is the form her husband so famously used. It is also appropriate that 'Anne Hathaway' is rich in **metaphor** since this is a figure beloved by Shakespeare. The metaphors at lines 8–9, 'I dreamed he'd written me', reflect Shakespeare's occupation, yet also indicate that his wife loves him so much that she desires to have been one of his creations.

The female **personae** in **'Havisham'** and **'The Laboratory'** are contrasting types, yet both are in the grip of a pathological obsession. Miss Havisham is tortured by the conflicting desires of love and hatred: 'Beloved sweetheart bastard' (line 1). She has erotic dreams about making love to her former lover that turn into castration fantasies: 'then down till I suddenly bite awake' (line 12). The woman in **'The Laboratory'** has turned her feelings of jealousy into a cold and calculating thirst for revenge: 'Which is the poison to poison her, prithee?' (line 4).

A masculine version of ruthless calculation can be found in the character of the Duke of Ferrara, narrator of **'My Last Duchess'**. Oddly enough, like the woman in **'The Laboratory'** who admires the old man's expertise in mixing the poisons to make them look harmless (lines 15 16), the Duke too has a great admiration for craftsmanship, especially when it involves making dead things look as if they were alive. Both are morally perverted, yet no other moral perspective is given in either **monologue.**

'Homecoming' by Simon Armitage can be seen as a kind of love poem. The final stanza implies an intimate relationship between the subject of the poem and the narrator, but the poem evades such a simple label. If it is a love poem, the emotions felt are mature and based on trust, for the girl has to trust the speaker to, as it were, allow her to step back into her past and put on the yellow jacket again. **'Homecoming'** is a fascinating poem to speculate upon. Why do you think it is called **'Homecoming'**? Maybe because her attempts at becoming an adult and forming relationships outside the home met with opposition and frustration, she has finally 'come home' by forming a trusting relationship with the narrator of the poem. Maybe the jacket represents some damage done to her emotional development when she was a teenager. Maybe the description of her body in terms of the jacket is an invitation to exist more happily within her self. Who knows? As the narrator says, 'you say which' (line 21).

Clare's '**Sonnet**' is a simple expression of love for the countryside in which the poet seems to be recording things as he sees them.

METHODS

Imagery

'**Havisham**' and '**The Laboratory**' contain some strong sensuous imagery. In the latter there is a contrast between the opulent imagery connected with wealth and privilege, the jewels that the speaker can bestow on the old man ('Now, take all my jewels, gorge gold to your fill', line 45), and the self-adorning objects which could be used to carry poison:

> To carry pure death in an earring, a casket,
> A signet, a fan-mount, a filigree basket!'   (lines 19–20)

Is Robert Browning making a connection between wealth and corruption? There is something exotic in the special names used to describe what is in the poisoner's laboratory and the jewels that are available to the speaker: 'mortar' (line 13), 'gum' (line 13), 'gold oozings' (line 14), 'phial' (line 15), 'lozenge' (line 21), 'pastille'(line 22).

In '**Havisham**' Carol Ann Duffy uses vivid colour imagery to suggest the woman's disturbed state of mind, her conflicting emotions of love, sexual obsession and hatred: 'I've dark green pebbles for eyes' (line 3), 'the dress / yellowing' (lines 6–7), 'Puce curses' (line 9), 'a white veil; a red balloon bursting' (line 13). What other kinds of emotions/states of mind might these colours suggest? Green, for example, is associated with both jealousy and naivety.

Sonnet form

'**Sonnet 130**' and '**Anne Hathaway**' make an obvious contrasting pair. It is certainly fruitful to compare two **sonnets** from two very different literary eras. Carol Ann Duffy's **rhyme** scheme is more relaxed than the traditional model developed by Shakespeare (*ababcdcdefefgg*); she uses the 'softer rhyme' referred to in line 5, i.e. **half-rhyme**. The **rhyming couplet** at the end does not introduce a new rhyme, as in Shakespeare, but returns to the idea of a physical relationship by recalling the word 'bed' used in line 8.

EXAMINER'S SECRET

Make sure you can spell the names of the authors you are writing about. Even though these are printed in the paper and the Anthology, each year a large number of candidates create a bad impression by misspelling names. Apart from anything else, it makes them look very inattentive.

Love is the dominant theme of the sonnet and both these sonnets have love as the essential theme. In each a strong statement about the subject occupies the first eight or so lines. **'Sonnet 130'**, however, contains a compressed and highly focused argument that develops through the three **quatrains** and culminates in the final **couplet**.

John Clare's **'Sonnet'** has fourteen lines but that is where the resemblance to traditional sonnet form ends! It is written in rhyming couplets, a simple technique which seems appropriate for Clare's naive attitude to his subject.

Ambiguity

At first glance, **'My Last Duchess'** is the account of a meeting between two aristocrats in which the Duke decides to show off a portrait of his late wife. The language of the Duke is polite and decorous – he addresses the envoy as 'Sir' (line 13) and 'you' (line 47) thus indicating the man's social inferiority – yet throughout the **monologue** Robert Browning employs language that is ambiguous for a situation that is full of **irony**. The pair are engaged in negotiations for the Duke's next marriage and by choosing to show the envoy the portrait of his 'last Duchess' (line 1) the Duke is not just showing off a possession, he is also implicitly revealing:

- His own attitude to women, which is that they have the same status as material possessions

- His brutal indifference

This technique of letting the character reveal, indirectly, his true self allows us to feel the awful story that exists underneath the surface of the poem. Browning achieves this by some strategic use of a grammatical technique called **ellipsis**, 'leaving out'. Look at the following quotations and try to supply what is missing:

'her looks went everywhere'   (line 24)

'I choose / Never to stoop'   (lines 42–3)

'I gave commands; / Then all smiles stopped together'   (lines 45–6)

 EXAMINER'S SECRET

If you find a poem ambiguous, don't be put off and think that you are not understanding the poem correctly. If you can back up what you say with quotations, the examiner will be impressed that you can make more than one interpretation.

DEATH

> ### Key poems
>
> | | |
> |---|---|
> | Simon Armitage | **November** |
> | Simon Armitage | **I've made out a will** |
> | Ben Jonson | **On my first Sonne** |
> | Charles Tichborne | **Tichborne's Elegy** |
> | Alfred Tennyson | **Ulysses** |

 DID YOU KNOW?

The mortality rate in seventeenth-century England was similar to that in some developing countries today.

IDEAS, ATTITUDES AND FEELINGS

'**On my first Sonne**' by Ben Jonson was written during a time when it was believed that everyone belonged to God and were only permitted to live in this world by Him. In this context, Jonson's 'I' expresses ideas and attitudes that were conventional for his time. In the seventeenth century, the mortality rate was high, especially among young children, and Jonson probably sincerely believed that his dead son was in a better place than this world and consequently should be genuinely envied (line 6). This does not detract from the genuine sense of grief and loss that exists within the poem. There is an obvious tension between the feelings Jonson feels he *should* be feeling and his natural sorrow as a father who has lost his first born son – 'O, could I loose all father, now' (line 5).

In Armitage's '**November**' we are firmly in the contemporary world where aging and death are seen as degrading and inevitable, with small hope of another, better existence afterwards. The poem describes the old people in the ward in terms of appalled disgust:

> In their pasty bloodless smiles,
> in their slack breasts, their stunned brains and their baldness,
> and in us John: we are almost these monsters.   (lines 7–9)

The last phrase makes the connection that saves the narrator from cruel detachment because that 'we' includes himself, the person addressed *and* the reader. Compared to Jonson's poem, the possibility of a better 'state' (line 6) saving the dead boy from the misery of 'fleshes rage' (line 7) and 'age' (line 8) does not exist here: for Armitage (and/or his narrator) the only consolation is the feeling of being alive when the sun (a traditional image for life and happiness) 'spangles ... / One thing we have to get, John, out of this life' (lines 16–17).

'I've made out a will' (Simon Armitage) and **'Tichborne's Elegy'** both reflect upon the approach of death, but in very different ways. In the Armitage poem the poet lists an inventory of his body parts; in **'Tichborne's Elegy'** the poem also takes the form of an inventory, but of many wider aspects of his life. Armitage's attitude to his body is that it is so much 'stock' (line 9), material goods of greater or lesser value, but still essentially material. Tichborne attempts to summarise his whole life, in both its abstract value and its physical. Of the two, **'I've made out a will'** is probably the most difficult, because death as such is not really the subject. Armitage is writing about his dead body, but at the same time he is placing his 'heart' as the central image of the poem. Why do you think this is? You might try to write down all the things you are likely to associate with the heart, the most obvious being 'love'. This is the normal subject of a **sonnet** and **'I've made out a will'** is written in a variation of this form. Do you think Armitage is suggesting something about love in this poem?

In Alfred Tennyson's **'Ulysses'** the hero does not expect to return from the one last journey he plans. This voyage, he knows, will end with his death, but this fills him with eager anticipation. He may one day meet again some of the old heroes of his youth: 'And see the great Achilles, whom we knew' (line 64). Ulysses' attitude to ageing and death is courageous and vital. As one critic has said, the poem 'represents the need to go onwards with life'. Rather than being resigned to a comfortable retirement with his 'agèd wife' (line 3) he still wants to experience fresh adventures, he is still as curious about the world as he was when most of his life was occupied by 'roaming with a hungry heart' (line 12). At the end of the poem the reader comes to realise how brave and stoical Ulysses is. The final lines emphasise this courage: 'strong in will / To strive, to seek, to find, and not to yield.' (lines 69–70).

CHECK THE BOOK

In Homer's *Odyssey* (Book 11) Ulysses actually does meet with Achilles when he visits the underworld.

METHODS

Use of first-person persona

All these poems use a first-person narrator. Only **'Ulysses'** can be said to be a **dramatic monologue,** in that it dramatises a specific character which is not the author and within which certain important things are revealed about the speaker. Remember that a first-person narrator allows the writer to:

● Reveal the speaker's private thoughts

● Create a feeling of intimacy between speaker and reader

● Create an **ironic** distance between the speaker's words and the real events sensed by the reader

Creation of tone

Tone implies that literature is like speech, requiring a speaker and a listener, 'tone' being the attitude of the speaker adopted to the listener. **'November'** and **'Tichborne's Elegy'** seem to have a rather despairing tone. The title of the first is enough to signal the mood of the poem. It builds up an atmosphere of weary fatalism through its attention to dull realistic detail – 'the badly parked car' (line 1), 'You check her towel, soap and family trinkets' (line 4). But it is the third line of the first stanza that sets the mood and therefore the tone of the whole poem: 'We have brought her here to die and we know it' (line 3).

The sense of a passage's tone is derived from the kind of **syntax** and vocabulary used. Read the third verse of **'November'** carefully and try to imagine the tone of voice required to communicate the speaker's emotions. 'Pasty' (line 7), 'slack' (line 8), 'stunned' (line 8), 'baldness' (line 8), 'monsters' (line 9) are all negative words with a concentration of sibilance (hissing 's' sounds). Do these indicate disgust, rage or fear? Or a mixture of emotions?

In **'Tichborne's Elegy'** tone is created through a series of simple statements that are all contradicted. In each case a good thing (e.g. 'My prime of youth', line 1) becomes a bad thing ('is but a frost of cares', line 1). Each of these contains a qualifier – a 'but' (line 1) or a 'yet' (line 5) – and this negative repetition builds up the feeling of despair that pervades the whole poem. Everything good is being cancelled out.

Ulysses' attitude can be guessed through a particular tone he uses in the references to his wife and to his son Telemachus (lines 3 and 33–43). On the surface, he obviously loves and appreciates the latter, but the placing of certain words and phrases makes the reader feel the prudent and 'decent' (line 40) Telemachus has not earned the ultimate respect of his adventurous father: 'He works his work, I mine' (line 43).

Time of day symbolising age or the passing of time

'The long day wanes'   ('**Ulysses**', line 55)

'The day is past, and yet I saw no sun' ('**Tichborne's Elegy**', line 5)

'Inside, we feel the terror of the dusk begin' ('**November**', line 13)

The use of times of day to signify the stages in life is a common **rhetorical** effect in literary language. In each of the above, death is equated with the end of the day, but for each speaker something different is meant or felt. In view of what has been said about tone, write some notes on each quotation suggesting how each poet uses this familiar symbolism differently. Don't forget to place the quotations within the context of the poems.

CHECK THE BOOK

The use of times of day to signify the stages of life goes back to classical literature. In Sophocles' *Oedipus Rex* (c 425 BC), the Sphinx asks the riddle 'What goes on four legs in the morning, two on noon, and three in the evening?'

VIOLENCE AND THREAT

Key poems

Carol Ann Duffy	**Education for Leisure**
Carol Ann Duffy	**Stealing**
Simon Armitage	**Hitcher**
Thomas Hardy	**The Man He Killed**
Robert Browning	**My Last Duchess**
Robert Browning	**The Laboratory**

IDEAS, ATTITUDES AND FEELINGS

'Hitcher' depicts a man who is deeply frustrated with his lot in life. He is tied to a job he clearly hates and which he is on the verge of losing – '*One more sick-note, mister, and you're finished. Fired*' (line 3). While driving his hired Vauxhall Astra (the make of the car places him as some kind of salesman) he picks up his opposite: a free-living, hippy student type whose brain is full of vague, sentimental ideals, obviously derived from listening to sixties folk singers like Bob Dylan – 'The truth, / he said, was blowin' in the wind, / or round the next bend' (lines 8–10). In one sense the poem depicts a clash between two very different value systems. We are told the hitcher was about the same age as the speaker and we can imagine two young men who have chosen different ways of life. The point is that one of them is carefree and the other not. What is interesting about this **monologue** is that we do not feel much sympathy for the hitcher, even though he has been viciously attacked and objectively he is the victim in the situation. He is wet, and from the point of view (which is all we have) of the hard-pushed wage slave, he is a scrounger 'hitching' a free lift through life.

Another poem that shows violent hatred and resentment is **'The Laboratory'**. Whereas Simon Armitage's speaker does not particularly gloat on the effects of his actions – the attack takes place casually, without even stopping the car – the Rococo lady of Robert Browning's poem takes a morbid interest in the effects of the poison she is having brewed. In this poem everything is calculation. She is convinced that having the power to kill her rivals (see line 22) will reverse her situation as a victim of what has happened. And she wants her particular rival to suffer: 'Let death be felt and the proof remain' (line 38).

The speaker's attitude towards suffering and death in **'The Man He Killed'** by Thomas Hardy is explicitly moral in a way that the Armitage and Browning poems are not. The death has been the result of random violence in warfare. The speaker, in a way, is as much the victim of circumstance because 'the man he killed' could just as easily have been him. A common ground is established between himself and his victim in the first stanza – 'Had he and I but met' (line 1) – and this capacity for identification with the dead soldier forms the whole poem. Compare the speaker's remark in **'Hitcher'**, 'We were the same age, give or take a week' (line 19), and reflect on how this is merely given as a neutral observation, without any feeling of sympathy.

A similar lack of empathy is sustained throughout **'My Last Duchess'** where the speaker's dislike for his late wife and lack of moral connection with the consequences of his 'commands' (line 45) makes the poem especially chilling. You might like to compare this poem with **'Stealing'** by Carol Ann Duffy. In each, something desired as a possession is destroyed when the speaker has become bored or angry. In each, the speaker is incapable of love.

There is also an implied attitude to the 'possession' of aesthetic objects in both these poems. The Duke is proud of his art collection but clearly it is there to reflect his wealth and power. The thief in **'Stealing'** appreciates the beauty of the moonlit snowman at first – 'He looked magnificent' (line 2) – but can only express this in terms of taking and destroying it when he discovers it 'didn't look the same' (line 17).

Destructiveness of a more pathological kind is examined in another of Duffy's poems, **'Education for Leisure'**. Here the intention to kill springs from an all-consuming vanity – 'I am a genius' (line 9). The speaker is a non-entity living on the outskirts of a town where he is on the dole, yet he has deluded himself into a feeling of power by killing a few living things around him in his home, a fly, a goldfish, possibly a budgie. His attitude to death is characterised by what he says after squashing the fly – 'and now the fly is in another language' (line 7). Death has no meaning for him and life has no purpose. He has only been educated for a wasteful leisure time.

 DID YOU KNOW?
Again we are assuming that the 'genius' is a male. What happens if we assume she is female?

METHODS

Simple diction/syntax

The speakers in the poems by Duffy and Armitage use a limited vocabulary and sentence construction. In **'Education for Leisure'**,

EXAMINER'S SECRET

The main focus of your answer in an exam should be on *how* the poet uses language to convey ideas, not on the ideas themselves without any reference to the text.

for example, this has a rather sinister effect because the speaker exists within a familiar domestic environment – note the goldfish, the cat, the budgie and '<u>our</u> bread-knife' (line 19) – and yet talks about grandiose things – 'I am going to play God' (line 3), '... today I am going to change the world' (line 10). The short, pared-down sentences indicate a mind that has difficulty making connections, or at least one that has a horribly over-simplified view of the world. (You might try contrasting the diction and syntax of this poem with that of **'Little Boy Lost/Found'** by William Blake, where the effect is completely different.)

Rhythm, regular and irregular

A poem written completely in regular rhythm runs smoothly, like clockwork. Modern poets generally combine regular and irregular lines in their poems to provide variety, dramatic contrasts, emphasis, or just to move the 'story' along. Simon Armitage employs both regular and irregular rhythms in **'Hitcher'**. 'I thumbed a lift to where the car was parked' (line 4) is a regular **iambic pentameter,** but the next line is irregular – 'A Vauxhall Astra. It was hired' (line 5). What effect do you think this has?

Enjambment

Enjambment is a line of poetry that is not **end-stopped** but runs on into the next line:

> I took a run
> and booted him. Again. Again.   ('**Stealing**', lines 17–18)

Here the enjambment enacts the meaning of the words; there is no time for the reader to pause and reflect. Notice that the important word 'run' is still placed at the end of the line, even though there is no end-stop.

Robert Browning makes considerable use of enjambment in **'My Last Duchess'**, the rhymes rarely falling at the end of a sentence and thus creating the effect of listening to what sounds like a real conversation.

Stanzas

'The Man He Killed' and 'The Laboratory' use stanzas in a very precise and formal manner with basic **rhyme** schemes (*abab* – 'The Man He Killed', *aabb* – 'The Laboratory'). Compare this kind of stanza and 'tight' rhyming scheme with Whitman's expansive single verse poem **'Patrolling Barnegat'**. Whitman's form reflects the broad sweep of his vision, the whole poem being one single sentence.

In **'The Man He Killed'** stanzas mark the stages of the speaker's argument, the first two and the last are self-contained. But between the third and fourth an enjambment occurs after the word 'although' (line 12) which leads to the clinching reason, provided in stanza four, why the soldier and the man he killed are alike. Robert Browning, in **'The Laboratory'**, uses stanza form and rhyme scheme to distance the subject matter from the reader. In any case, there is something bizarre about using rather jaunty **couplets** to express the feelings and ideas of a poisoner!

DID YOU KNOW?

The word 'stanza' in Italian means 'room'. In what way does a stanza resemble a room?

Now take a break!

PART FOUR

RESOURCES

HOW TO USE QUOTATIONS

One of the secrets of success in writing essays is the way you use quotations. There are five basic principles:

❶ Put inverted commas at the beginning and end of the quotation.

❷ Write the quotation exactly as it appears in the original.

❸ Do not use a quotation that repeats what you have just written.

❹ Use the quotation so that it fits into your sentence.

❺ Keep the quotation as short as possible.

EXAMINER'S SECRET
Memorise one useful quote from each of the poems you are studying. It could be the word, phrase or line that you think is the most important.

Quotations should be used to develop the line of thought in your essays. Your comment should not duplicate what is in your quotation. For example:

> **Margaret ends by saying that she has no friend on earth: 'I have no other earthly friend' (line 77).**

Far more effective is to write:

> **Margaret ends by saying 'I have no other earthly friend' (line 77).**

Always lay out the lines as they appear in the text. For example:

> **Blake's lines often have a symbolic power and simplicity: 'The mire was deep, and the child did weep, / And away the vapour flew' (lines 7–8).**

Or:

> **'The mire was deep, and the child did weep,**
> **And away the vapour flew'** (lines 7–8).

However, the most sophisticated way to use the writer's words is to embed them into your sentence:

> **When the Duke says that he 'gave commands; / Then all smiles stopped together' (lines 45–6) we are shocked by his ruthlessness.**

SITTING THE EXAMINATION

Examination papers are carefully designed to give you the opportunity to do your best. Follow these handy hints for exam success:

BEFORE YOU START

- Make sure you know the subject of the examination so that you are properly prepared and equipped.

- You need to be comfortable and free from distractions. Inform the invigilator if anything is off-putting, e.g. a shaky desk.

- Read the instructions, or rubric, on the front of the examination paper. You should know by now what you have to do but check to reassure yourself.

- Observe the time allocation – and follow it carefully. If they recommend 60 minutes for Question 1 and 30 minutes for Question 2, it is because Question 1 carries twice as many marks.

- Consider the mark allocation. You should write a longer response for 4 marks than for 2 marks.

WRITING YOUR RESPONSES

- Use the questions to structure your response, e.g. question: 'The endings of X's poems are always particularly significant. Explain their importance with reference to two poems.' The first part of your answer will describe the ending of the first poem; the second part will look at the ending of the second poem; the third part will be an explanation of the significance of the two endings.

 **EXAMINER'S SECRET**
You will not be marked on your rough notes as long as you indicate clearly that is what they are. The marker will be pleased to see evidence of planning and reflection.

- Write a brief draft outline of your response.

- A typical 30-minute examination essay is probably between 400 and 600 words in length.

- Keep your writing legible and easy to read, using paragraphs to show the structure of your answers.

- Spend a couple of minutes afterwards quickly checking for obvious errors.

WHEN YOU HAVE FINISHED

- Don't be downhearted – if you found the examination difficult, it is probably because you really worked at the questions. Let's face it, they are not meant to be easy!

- Don't pay too much attention to what your friends have to say about the paper. Everyone's experience is different and no two people ever give the same answers.

EXAMINER'S SECRET

Note the difference between *compare* and *contrast*. The first means focus on points of similarity; the second means focus on differences. Of course, when you *compare* you will be taking into consideration differences between poem A and poem B; when you *contrast* you will be recognising similarities. It's a question of emphasis. Show the marker you understand this distinction in your answers.

IMPROVE YOUR GRADE

HOW TO SELECT THE POEMS

In the exam, one poem from one of the two modern poets, or from the pre-1914 selection, will be nominated in each question and you will be free to choose three other poems for the purposes of comparison.

You must write about at least one poem from each of the modern poets. At least two other poems must be chosen from the selection of pre-1914 poems.

- Read the named poem in the question carefully and reflect on the best poem to match it with from the other modern poet. Ask yourself two basic questions:

  - What is the poem about?

  - What methods are used?

- The given poem may be described briefly in some way in the question. Regard this as a clue to the poems that you will choose.

  For example, '**Education for Leisure**' (Carol Ann Duffy) is named and described as 'disturbing'. A possible pairing would be with '**Hitcher**' (Simon Armitage) because:

  - Both poems are **dramatic monologues**
  - Both feature violent and frustrated characters/speakers

- Having decided on two modern poems you should think carefully about a pair of appropriate pre-1914 poems. If you feel that the form of the poem is going to be your guide, then an opportunity to analyse contrasting techniques within the dramatic monologue could be found by selecting Robert Browning's '**The Laboratory**'. This would also enable you to compare and contrast the different styles poets adopt for male and female speakers. The female speaker in '**The Laboratory**' is very different from the other would-be killer in Duffy's '**Education for Leisure**'. Finally, another pre-1914 monologue that is related to the violent and disturbing theme could be '**The Man He Killed**' by Thomas Hardy. Here the perspective of the speaker is very different from the others, thus offering further opportunities for contrasts to be made.

- Another question might nominate one of the pre-1914 poems. It may ask you to consider poems where the use of form, structure and language shapes the meaning. '**Sonnet 130**' by William Shakespeare is nominated. You could choose Carol Ann Duffy's '**Anne Hathaway**' to go with this for the obvious reason that it is a **sonnet** about Shakespeare, yet one that does not strictly adhere to the 'Shakespearean' sonnet form. This would be a chance to contrast the different technical approaches. Simon Armitage has also written in a variation of the sonnet form, so any of the four poems from *A Book of Matches* could be used here, i.e. '**Mother, any distance**', '**My father thought it bloody queer**', '**I've made out a will**' and '**Those bastards in their mansions**'. Finally, to keep the focus on the sonnet, you could examine John Clare's '**Sonnet**'. Thus a form that is notable for its structure could be the starting point for your answer.

EXAMINER'S SECRET

To achieve a grade B you must write about at least four poems. It is impossible to gain a grade higher than a C if you only write about three poems, however good your answer.

EXAMINER'S SECRET

The sonnet is an obvious choice when asked to write about structure. However, all poems have some kind of structure even when it is not at all formal or obvious. You will gain marks if you are able to write with sensitivity about a variety of different types of structure.

- Another question might ask you to compare the ways that poets write about death. **'November'** by Simon Armitage is nominated. You choose **one** poem by Carol Ann Duffy and at least **two** from the pre-1914 poetry bank. Think of the links that can be made with **'November'**. There is **'Ulysses'** by Alfred Tennyson, which reveals profoundly different attitudes to aging and dying. **'Tichborne's Elegy'** by Charles Tichborne articulates a fear of death in a despairing **tone** that can be compared to the one Armitage uses. From Carol Ann Duffy's poems you might be able to use **'We Remember Your Childhood Well'** by interpreting 'death' metaphorically and writing about the *death* of innocence which features in the **subtext** of this poem.

HOW TO CONSTRUCT A RESPONSE

The question

Although each question in your choice of questions will be worded differently, and with a different emphasis, the examiner will be looking to reward the same kind of things whatever you choose to write about. The examination board specifies criteria which, when put more simply, boil down to three basic things:

- The different approaches to the topic specified by the question (e.g. death, love, emotions, parent and child attitudes etc.)

- The different language styles used by the poets

- The different intended effects on you the reader of each poem

If you focus on these three things in your answers you will be successful, however difficult you find writing exam answers on poetry.

Taking the question apart

Before you start to write anything, look at the question carefully and identify the important bits.

Here is a typical question:

> **Compare the ways poets present powerful emotions in at least four of the poems you have studied. Write about 'Havisham'**

by Carol Ann Duffy, one poem by Simon Armitage, and two from the Pre-1914 Poetry Bank.

Underline key words in the question so that you can refer to them easily:

EXAMINER'S SECRET

To achieve full flexibility in your examination choices, make sure you study all eight poems by each of your chosen modern poets.

> Compare the ways poets present powerful emotions in at least four of the poems that you have studied. Write about 'Havisham' by Carol Ann Duffy, **one** poem by Simon Armitage, and **two** from the Pre-1914 Poetry Bank.

- **Powerful Emotions** is what your answer must be about, which means **you can write about any kind of 'powerful emotion'**, not just the obvious one!

- **Compare the ways** is what you are instructed to do. This means you must write about **the ways the poets use language.**

- **Four of the poems** – if you write about **fewer than four you will lose marks.**

The answer

First, you must select one poem by Simon Armitage that features powerful emotions. Since **'Havisham'** is about a bitter and sexually frustrated woman, you might want to select, by way of a contrast, a poem like **'Mother, any distance'**, a poem about the powerful bond between the speaker and his mother and the equally strong impulse to break free.

Two pre-1914 poems to go with the above could be:

- **'The Affliction of Margaret'** by William Wordsworth, a poem about the powerful feelings of a mother for her lost son.

- **'On my first Sonne'** by Ben Jonson would complete the four poems on 'powerful emotions' since it is an elegy on the death of his beloved son.

Now that you have chosen the poem you will write about, you need to think about how you will **structure** your answer. This often

EXAMINER'S SECRET

Refer to the speaking voice in the poem as 'the speaker' or 'the poet'. For example, do not write, '**In this poem, Wordsworth says that Margaret's son was "well born, well bred"**'. However, you can write, .'**In this poem, Wordsworth presents a speaker who...**'

EXAMINER'S SECRET

Use the **present tense** when writing your answer. The poem, as a work of literature, still exists!

poses problems in a question requiring some kind of comparison. There are many valid approaches, but you must never write about one poem after another in separate paragraphs. **You need to work out a strategy well in advance of the exam!** (See **Sample essay plan**.)

Here are three examples, with grade criteria, of three different standards of response to the above question. (Note that the examples do not represent complete answers.)

Grade F – Criteria and response

In their responses, candidates:

- Show knowledge of what is in the poems

- Comment on ideas and the different ways the poems are presented

- Make basic links between the poems

- Describe their own personal responses

A grade-F candidate might respond to a question as follows:

The woman in 'Havisham' is angry about how she has been treated. She wants to kill the man who let her down – 'Give me a male corpse for a long slow honeymoon'. [*This shows knowledge of what is in the poem.*] The poem is written in stanzas of four lines and there is a lot of reference to colours in the words Carol Ann uses. Example – '*Puce curses*' which makes you think of how angry she was. [*This is a comment on the way the poem is presented, and it gives a personal response.*] This is an example of an image, like the one in 'Mother, any distance' that shows the idea of freedom – 'the prairies of the floors'. [*This makes a basic link between poems.*] This poem by Simon Armitage is a sonnet. In the poem Simon writes about how his mother helps him but he feels he wants to be free and independent. There are powerful emotions in 'The Affliction of Margaret' too because the lady in this poem has lost her only son and has no 'earthly friend'. Her situation is worse than Ben Jonson's in 'On my first Sonne' because he at least knows that his son is dead and has escaped the 'miserie' of life. [*This too makes a basic link between poems.*]

Grade C – Criteria and response

In their responses, candidates:

- Focus on feelings, attitudes and ideas in the poems

- Cross-reference to show similarities or differences between the poems

- Use details from the poems to support their views and demonstrate poetic technique

- Show some understanding of cultural contexts

- Develop their own personal responses

A grade-C candidate might respond to a question as follows:

'Havisham' describes the character of Miss Havisham from *Great Expectations* by Charles Dickens. [*This shows some understanding of cultural contexts.*] **She is a woman who has been jilted on her wedding day. The poem begins with the sentence 'Beloved sweetheart bastard' which tells us how the speaker's feelings have changed for her former lover.** [*This focuses on a feeling in the poem and uses a detail in the poem to demonstrate poetic technique.*] **Later in the second verse we learn that she is full of self-disgust at being an unmarried old woman – 'Spinster. I stink and remember'. The feelings Duffy shows are all negative, even when she has a pleasant dream about making love to her former lover it ends with her imagining she is castrating him – 'I bite awake'. Powerful emotions are conveyed by the vivid colour imagery Duffy uses, like 'a red balloon bursting in my face' which shows the sudden shock of her happiness coming to an end.** [*This focuses on a feeling in the poem and uses a detail in the poem to demonstrate poetic technique.*] **The speaker seems to be trapped in time, she can't 'move on' – 'whole days in bed cawing Nooooo at the wall'. This contrasts to the emotions of the**

EXAMINER'S SECRET

Some **verbs** you can use when writing about poems:

presents / illustrates / characterises / portrays / contrasts / suggests / implies / shows.

poet in 'Mother any distance' who wants to escape being tied to his mother yet doesn't know if he can survive on his own – 'I reach towards a hatch that opens on an endless sky to fall or fly'. [*This is a cross-reference to show a difference between the poems.*] Simon seems to be uncertain of himself in this poem, yet he knows that his mother is important to him – she is the 'anchor' to his 'kite'. There are powerful feelings too in 'The Affliction of Margaret' and 'On my first Sonne'. Both the poems are about parents who have lost their children. Whereas the other two poems are about complicated feelings, these two express something very simple, grief.

Grade A – Criteria and response

In their responses, candidates:

- Explore and empathise with the poems' ideas

- Use quotations that are integrated into their arguments

- Analyse poetic techniques and their effectiveness

- Make explicit comparisons and note contrasts between the poems

- Recognise the literary tradition and the social/cultural contexts of the poems

- Show an awareness of a variety of possible interpretations and develop a strong personal evaluation

Powerful personal emotions are apparent in 'Havisham' from the very first sentence – 'Beloved sweetheart bastard'. These three nouns act as a kind of history of her relationship with the man, from the formal 'beloved' through the more intimate 'sweetheart' to the explosion of hatred in 'bastard'. Also, the fact that the sentence is verbless and unpunctuated adds to the sense of conflicting feelings all existing at the same time. The alliterations of 'beloved' and 'bastard' give the sentence its aggression; there is a similarity between the words that suggests how easily and quickly 'beloved' became 'bastard'. [*This shows an awareness of a variety of possible interpretations.*]

DID YOU KNOW?

The word 'essay' comes from the Latin 'exigere', meaning 'to weigh' or 'to balance'.

Havisham's intense and bitter hatred is caused by her sense of rejection. She is humiliated because she is a 'Spinster'. Duffy isolates this word in a single sentence to imply the feelings of social shame and loneliness attached to the condition. The next sentence sums up the awful state of obsession that grips her – 'I stink and remember'. 'Stink' has connotations of something animal and neglected, an idea that is taken up by the phrase 'Whole days / in bed cawing Nooooo at the wall'. She is like a mad parrot trapped in a cage, repeating the same sounds over and over again. [*This shows exploration of and empathy with the poem's ideas.*]

On a less explicit level, the feelings of being driven by strong emotions are examined in Simon Armitage's 'Mother, any distance'. [*This analyses one of the poet's techniques and its effectiveness and makes a comparison between the texts.*] Here the poet/speaker is 'rising' in the world while still symbolically attached to his mother – 'I space-walk through the empty bedrooms, climb / the ladder to the loft, to breaking point, where something / has to give'. The whole poem moves towards a final bid for freedom represented by the image of the hatch in the roof opening 'on an endless sky / to fall or fly'. Armitage uses an ordinary situation and ordinary language to convey the feelings of a young person trying to establish his own identity separate to his parent. He still needs to 'find his feet' as an adult – 'I space-walk through the empty bedrooms' gives the feeling of uncertainty in a new environment; his mother still holds on to her son – 'your fingertips still pinch / the last one-hundreth of an inch' hints at her determination not to let go.

The mother in 'The Affliction of Margaret', however, had let go of her son when he was at an early age and now yearns to find out what has happened to him. Like Duffy's 'Havisham' this is a dramatic monologue in which a distressed psychological state is evoked. Margaret's 'apprehensions come in crowds' and she is completely friendless. Wordsworth builds up a picture of Margaret's 'affliction' in language that for its time would have been considered simple and direct. [*This recognises the literary tradition and the social context of the poem.*] The three

WWW. CHECK THE NET http://www. simonarmitage.co. uk/. This contains a wide range of interviews, reviews and information on the poet.

DID YOU KNOW?

English teachers in East Yorkshire refused to teach *Education for Leisure* by Carol Anne Duffy because of its violent content.

full-rhymes that complete each of the stanzas create an almost nursery- rhyme effect, as if the speaker's preoccupation with her child has influenced her way of speaking. Ben Jonson in 'On my first Sonne' also employs simple straightforward language, even though the ideas and feelings behind the words are complex. The last two lines, for example, compress a complicated idea into a simple rhyming couplet: 'For whose sake, hence-forth, all his vows be such, / As what he loves may never like too much'. That is, the hope that whoever he loves from now on, he may never become too attached to.

SAMPLE ESSAY PLAN

To help with your revision and your planning here is a sample question and answer. Remember, this does not represent the only answer to this question. This is merely one suggestion. Do not forget either that this is only an outline.

QUESTION

Compare *at least four* poems from those you have studied where strong dislike for another person is shown. Write about 'My Last Duchess' by Robert Browning, *one* poem by Carol Ann Duffy, *one* poem by Simon Armitage, and *one* other poem from the Pre-1914 Poetry Bank.

Poems

- 'My Last Duchess' by Robert Browning

- 'Havisham' by Carol Ann Duffy

- 'Hitcher' by Simon Armitage

- 'The Laboratory' by Robert Browning

Paragraph 1

The first paragraph should present in general terms the way the theme of 'strong dislike for another' applies to the four poems:

- 'My Last Duchess' by Robert Browning shows the Duke's dislike of his former wife.

- 'The Laboratory' by Robert Browning shows the lady's dislike and hatred of the woman who has taken her lover from her.

- 'Havisham' by Carol Ann Duffy shows the speaker's dislike of her former lover.

- 'Hitcher' by Simon Armitage is different to the others in that it is not about dislike related to sexual relationships. It shows the speaker's dislike of the 'hitcher's' attitudes and philosophy of life.

- You might like to note here that the poems represent two male speakers and two female and that they are all **dramatic monologues**.

- For each poem, make sure that you comment on the particular feature that the examiners ask for (such as here where 'strong dislike is shown'). Briefly state what each poem is about, both obviously on the surface and at a deeper level.

Paragraph 2

The next two paragraphs should begin to develop the answer in a more specific way by focusing in more detail on the themes, the ideas, attitudes and feelings presented in the poems. These could be:

- The contrast between the male speakers in 'My Last Duchess' and 'Hitcher', and their different feelings of dislike. In both characters the feeling of dislike leads to a violent act that gets rid of the disliked or hated person. You could contrast the motivation of each character, arguing perhaps that the Duke is motivated by pride and vanity, the speaker in 'Hitcher' by resentment and possibly jealousy.

Paragraph 3

- 'The Laboratory' and 'Havisham' feature two women who fantasise about acts of revenge on the men who have rejected them. In the former the speaker makes much of the effects of the poison upon her rival – 'Brand, burn up, bite into its grace' (line 39); in the latter the hatred is more psychological and implicit –

 DID YOU KNOW?

In 1999 Duffy was thought to be a serious contender for the post of Poet Laureate in view of her apparent popularity with ordinary readers. However, Prime Minister Tony Blair opted for a less adventurous candidate, Professor Andrew Motion.

DID YOU KNOW?

Duffy enjoys playing poker and watching football – she supports Liverpool – and watches *Coronation Street.*

'I suddenly bite awake' (line 12). You could expand on their different moods – almost ecstatic at the opportunity to take revenge in the Browning poem, and grimly murderous – 'Give me a male corpse' (line 15) – in the Duffy.

In the next two paragraphs you could explore how the poets use language and form to communicate the feelings of dislike.

Paragraph 4

- With **'My Last Duchess'** and **'Hitcher'** you could compare the ways a **first-person persona** is created. Both poets for example use the first person, yet the person addressed is different in each. In **'My Last Duchess'** it is an envoy with whom the Duke is negotiating the dowry for his next duchess; in **'Hitcher'** the addressee is non-specific or just the reader. How do the speakers 'reveal' themselves to the reader?

- It would be appropriate to discuss the use of **tone** here. How do Armitage and Browning convey attitudes through the tone of phrases like 'He was following the sun to west from east' (**'Hitcher'**, line 7) and 'She had a heart – how shall I say? – too soon made glad' (**'My Last Duchess'**, lines 21–2)?

- Both poets use a **colloquial register** to give the flavour of an actual speaker. Compare some examples from each poem.

- You also might want to consider the use of **enjambment** in each poem, the way it allows the speech to flow on taking the reader with it.

- Both poets use **rhyme**. In Browning's case the **heroic couplets** never interrupt the movement of the narrative, and Armitage uses **half-** and **internal rhymes** in a similarly unobtrusive way.

What other formal elements could you discuss here?

Paragraph 5

- Like the other two poems a first-person persona is created in each. The speaker in the **'The Laboratory'** is addressing the 'old man' (line 46) as he mixes the poison. Therefore as in **'My Last Duchess'** a particular scene and situation is implied.

'Havisham', like 'Hitcher', is not addressed to any specific person. Does the first-person narrative intensify the sense of dislike and hatred in the poems?

- The **rhythm** of 'The Laboratory' seems to be at odds with its subject matter. Each stanza presents a complete idea or stage in the narrative separately with a full-stop at the end. How does this compare with 'Havisham', which does not have a rhyming scheme and has stanzas that are linked by enjambment?

- 'The Laboratory' and 'Havisham' contain some strong, sensuous **imagery**. Contrast the different effects of this, for example the colour imagery in 'Havisham' reflects certain emotional states such as jealousy. In 'The Laboratory' there is the imagery of wealth and voluptuousness that evokes the social status and moral world of the speaker and her circle.

DID YOU KNOW?

When asked why poetry mattered in the world, Duffy replied 'Perhaps poetry can articulate ordinary people's feelings and worries and in some way be a form of consolation or utterance for common humanity – very much in that way as a form of unholy prayer.'

Paragraph 6

This paragraph could include some ideas about the cultural and literary context of the poems. The Browning and Duffy poems are all set in a previous time to which they were written. Does this influence the way we read them? For example, the word 'Spinster' ('Havisham', line 5) is hardly used today, and an unmarried woman is not stigmatised in the way she would have been in the nineteenth century. Is Duffy saying something about women in the past, or are the feelings expressed in the poem universal? You might also like to include some reference to the way the speaker and the hitchhiker in 'Hitcher' might represent two different attitudes to life – the one a frustrated wage slave, the other a free-wheeling hippy type justifying his existence with clichéd thinking derived from sixties folk songs.

Conclusion

Conclude by summarising what you have argued, but try not to reiterate everything you have said in the main body of your essay. Refer to a key word from the question if you can – this shows that you have answered it!

FURTHER QUESTIONS

These suggested examination questions are presented in the sort of format that is used in the examinations and use the broad themes that are discussed in these Notes. They are not intended to be either complete or exclusive and of course other words could be used to identify a topic that is very close to these here.

1 'Those bastards in their mansions' could be described as an angry poem. Do you agree? Make clear the reasons for your response, and compare this poem with **at least three** of the other poems you have studied which contain feelings of anger. At least **one** of these should be by Carol Ann Duffy, and **two** from the Pre-1914 Poetry Bank.

2 Compare the ways in which the poets present women in **four or more** of the poems you have studied, including at least one by each poet. You should write about 'Havisham' by Carol Ann Duffy, and compare it with at least **one** poem by Simon Armitage, and **two** poems from the Pre-1914 Poetry Bank.

3 Compare **at least four** of the poems you have studied where parent-child feelings are shown. Write about 'On my first Sonne', **one** poem by Carol Ann Duffy, **one** poem by Simon Armitage, and **one** other poem from the Pre-1914 Poetry Bank.

4 Compare the ways in which poets present men in **four or more** of the poems you have studied. You should write about 'My father thought it bloody queer' by Simon Armitage, and compare it with at least **one** poem by Carol Ann Duffy, and **two** poems from the Pre-1914 Poetry Bank.

5 Compare the ways poets present strong emotions in **four or more** of the poems you have studied. Write about 'The Laboratory' by Robert Browning, **one** poem by Carol Ann Duffy, **one** poem by Simon Armitage and **one** other poem from the Pre-1914 Poetry Bank.

6 'Elvis's Twin Sister' by Carol Ann Duffy is an amusing poem, unlike most you have studied in the Anthology. Did you enjoy reading it? Compare it with **at least three** other poems you have

EXAMINER'S SECRET

Leave ten minutes at the end of the exam to read over everything you have written.

studied, making it clear why you did or did not enjoy them.
Include **one** poem by Simon Armitage and **two** poems from the
Pre-1914 Poetry Bank.

7 Death features in several of the poems you have studied.
Compare the ways poets write about death **in at least four** of
the poems. Write about '**November**' by Simon Armitage, **one**
poem by Carol Ann Duffy, and **two** poems from the Pre-1914
Poetry Bank.

8 Compare the ways poets use form, structure and language to
convey emotions and ideas in **four** poems you have studied. You
should write about '**Sonnet 130**' by Shakespeare, **one** poem by
Carol Ann Duffy, **one** poem by Simon Armitage, and **one** other
poem from the Pre-1914 Poetry Bank.

9 Compare the ways poets write about love in **four of the poems**
you have studied. You should write about '**Before You Were
Mine**' by Carol Ann Duffy, **one** poem by Simon Armitage, and
two poems from Pre-1914 Poetry Bank.

10 Compare the ways poets write about violence and/or violent
characters in **four of the poems** you have studied. You should
write about '**Hitcher**' by Simon Armitage, **one** poem by Carol
Ann Duffy, and **two** poems from the Pre-1914 Poetry Bank.

**EXAMINER'S
SECRET**

Try the technique of
visualisation before
you start to answer
the question.
Imagine you are
writing your exam
paper with all your
thoughts smoothly
falling into place
and you're
completely in
control of what you
are doing. This
technique will help
you calm down and
produce the best
work you can.

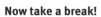 **Now take a break!**

allegory a story or situation written in such a way as to have two coherent meanings

alliteration a sequence of repeated sounds in a stretch of language

ambiguity the capacity of words and sentences to have double meanings

anapaest a trisyllabic metrical foot, consisting of two unstressed syllables followed by a stressed syllable – ti-ti-tum

antithetic parallelisms opposing or contrasting ideas in next-door sentences or clauses

assonance the correspondence, or near correspondence, in two words of the stressed vowel, e.g. can and fat, child and silence

atmosphere a mood or feeling that dominates a poem

blank verse unrhymed **iambic pentameter** – a line of five lines

blazon a description of a woman's beauty in list form

cadenced the rhythm of prose or verse caused by the various stresses placed on syllables and words

caesura a pause within a line of verse

cliché a boring phrase or word, made tedious by frequent repetition

colloquialism expressions and grammar associated with ordinary, everyday speech

conceit a special sort of **figurative** device, usually a **simile** which compares two apparently dissimilar things

connotation the secondary meanings of a word, what it suggests or implies

consonant speech sound combined with vowel to form syllable

couplet a pair of rhymed lines of any **metre**

decorum use of the proper and fitting style for every literary kind

diction the choice of words in a work of literature

dramatic monologue a poem in which a specific person, not the poet, is speaking

elegy a poem lamenting the death of a particular person

ellipsis in grammar the omission of words thought to be essential in the complete form of the sentence

end-stopped verse a line of verse in which the end of the line coincides with an essential pause

enjambment a line of poetry that is not **end-stopped**, in which the sentence continues into the next line

epic a long narrative poem about the exploits of super-human heroes or gods

epigraphs quotation or fragment placed at the beginning of poems, chapters or novels as a clue to their meaning

epitaph an inscription on a tomb, or piece of writing suitable for that purpose

euphemism word or phrase that is less blunt or terrifying, e.g. 'pass away' = die

euphony language that sounds pleasant and musical

figurative language any form of expression or grammar that departs from the plainest expression of meaning

first-person persona the speaker/narrator in poem or story who is clearly not the author

free verse verse released from the conventions of metre with its regular pattern of stress and line lengths

half-rhyme an imperfect rhyme

heroic couplet lines of **iambic pentameters** rhymed in pairs

iamb a weak stress followed by a strong stress, ti-tum

iambic pentameter a line of five **iambic** feet

idiom expression or usage peculiar to a language

image a picture which words create in the mind of a reader

imagery any **figurative language** (metaphors and **similes**)

internal rhyme a pair of words rhyming within a line of verse, e.g. "Fleas. / Adam ad 'em"

irony saying one thing while you mean another

Italian sonnet fourteen line Italian sonnet rhymed *abbaabba, cdecde* (or *cdcdcd*).

masculine rhyme a monosyllabic rhyme on the final stressed syllable of two lines of verse

metaphor a metaphor is when two different things are fused together; one thing described as another thing

metre the pattern of stressed and unstressed syllables in a line of verse

monologue single person speaking with or without an audience is uttering a monologue

motif dominant/recurring idea or theme in literary or musical composition

myth story usually concerning super-humans or gods

onomatopoeia words which sound like the noise which they describe

octave first eight lines of a sonnet

oxymoron a figure of speech in which contrasting terms are brought together

paradoxical an apparently self-contradictory statement. Absurdity

persona in novels or poems the point of view of a person who is clearly not the author

pun a play on words

quatrain a verse or group of four lines

realism the representation of 'ordinary' life

refrain recurring phrase or line at end of stanza

register a kind of language being used appropriate to a situation

rhetorical persuasive language

rhyme the deliberate matching of sounds that creates an audible attern

rhyming couplet two-line rhyme

rhythm in poetry the chief element of rhythm is the variation in levels of stress accorded to the syllables

Shakespearean sonnet fourteen line English sonnet rhymed *abab, cdcd, efef, gg*

simile a figure of speech in which one thing is said to be like another

sonnet a fourteen-line poem written to one of a number of established patterns

stereotype conventional idea or image of character or thing

subtext a word for the situation that lies behind the behaviour of the characters in a play

symbol something which represents something else

synonym word with same meaning as another

syntax the arrangement of words in their appropriate forms and proper order

tabloidese language typical of tabloid newspapers

tone the sense of a particular mood or manner in which a passage should be read

tragic in literature, it is 'tragic' when an individual experiences a downfall as a result of both their strengths and their weaknesses

vernacular language or dialect of particular class or group

CHECKPOINT HINTS/ANSWERS

CHECKPOINT 1 Perhaps the words 'Whole days / in bed cawing Nooooo at the wall' (lines 5-6) characterise her obsession and loneliness best. She has become a kind of animal, howling or repeating the same word over and over again, like a parrot trapped in a cage.

CHECKPOINT 2 Duffy's imagery is very modern and diverse. She can use two widely different images side by side to make an unexpected connection between them.

CHECKPOINT 3 Shakespeare himself adapted the form and wrote 154 love sonnets. None were addressed to his wife, though.

CHECKPOINT 4 'Elvis's Twin Sister' makes a good contrasting poem because they are totally different types of women.

CHECKPOINT 5 Duffy enjoys the dramatic effect of one-word sentences – compare 'Spinster' (line 5) in 'Havisham' – and here the single word produces a thoughtful, nostalgic and affectionate pause in the flow of the writing. Her mother and the famous star become one for a moment.

CHECKPOINT 6 The character Gloucester in King Lear, says 'As flies to wanton boys are we to the gods... They kill us for their sport' (Act IV). The persona in the poem decides to play God and kill someone.

CHECKPOINT 7 In this poem 'breaking point' at line 10 refers to the strain put on the unreeling tape measure, the suppressed kite image, and the relationship between mother and son.

CHECKPOINT 8 The parental roles are to an extent stereotypes. The mother is depicted as helpful and supportive; while the father comes across as disapproving and critical.

CHECKPOINT 9 The poem depicts the consequences of coming home late at night and also reveals the sense of a present 'homecoming', in which the poet invites the girl to 'step backwards' (line 21) again into her past.

CHECKPOINT 10 A spangle is only a small speck of light. As if the sun only provides us humans with a small and possibly illusory reason to 'feel alive' (line 16).

CHECKPOINT 11 'Stops or hangs' could mean that either when he dies everything stops, including the essence of his being; or if you emphasise the word 'hang', then some part will continue to exist, 'hanging' as it were like a picture in a gallery.

CHECKPOINT 12 In his use of strong Anglo-Saxon diction, his obviously deep love and understanding of literary forms, Simon Armitage is closest to Jonson.

CHECKPOINT 13 The metre is heavily stressed and can be clearly heard when the poem is read aloud. It is a combination of iambs ('I rise') and anapests ('In the dawn').

CHECKPOINT 14 The poem contains examples of what, in its time, would have been considered ordinary speech ('I dread the rustling of the grass', line 65) 'I question things', line 68). Wordsworth rejected conventional poetic language and preferred to use 'a selection of language really used by men' ('Preface to Lyrical Ballads').

CHECKPOINT 15 The fact that it was written just before the young Tichborne was horribly executed must make it especially moving to the reader.

CHECKPOINT 16 Tichborne does use a repeated metaphorical device throughout the poem, but the repetition could be said to increase the sense of a doomed young man 'adding up' what his life means.

CHECKPOINT 17 With a very ironic tone of voice!

CHECKPOINT 18 Whitman combines both the effects of **alliteration** and **onomatopoeia** in phrases like 'slush and sand' (line 6) and 'swirl and spray' (line 8) to communicate the physical effects of the storm and the shore.

CHECKPOINT 19 They would probably respond to the honesty of a poem that stresses their appeal as a real person.

CHECKPOINT 20 She was innocent and lively, unaware of the affect she was having on her husband.

CHECKPOINT 21 In order to stress his reasonable nature. After all he is negotiating a new marriage.

CHECKPOINT 22 It now gives him complete control over her. Also he regards his art collection as his own property to be made and to be viewed on his own terms. See the last word of the poem.

CHECKPOINTS 23 It shows how excited the woman is at the prospect of revenge.

CHECKPOINT 24 She wants to believe that her lover was trapped by this other woman, that he did not desert her of his own choice.

CHECKPOINT 25 It means death.

CHECKPOINT 26 He has a very low opinion of them. He thinks he is far more sophisticated than they are.

CHECKPOINT 27 The fact that he knew lots of long words that sounded impressive.

CHECKPOINT 28 Claws. They are suggested by the hard 'c' sounds.

CHECKPOINT 29 Possibly in the image of the horse in the first line.

CHECKPOINT 30 The word that is repeated at the beginning of some of the lines is 'I'.

CAROL ANN DUFFY

1 Anne Hathaway

2 Elvis's Twin Sister

3 Havisham

4 Before You Were Mine

5 Salome

6 Stealing

7 We Remember Your Childhood Well

8 Education for Leisure

SIMON ARMITAGE

1 Mother, any distance

2 Homecoming

3 My father thought it bloody queer

4 November

5 Those bastards in their mansions

6 Kid

7 Hitcher

8 I've made out a will

PRE-1914 POETRY BANK

1 The Song of the Old Mother (W. B. Yeats)

2 The Affliction of Margaret (William Wordsworth)

3 Tichborne's Elegy (Charles Tichborne)

4 Sonnet 130 (William Shakespeare)

5 The Village Schoolmaster (Oliver Goldsmith)

6 Inversnaid (Gerard Manley Hopkins)

7 Sonnet (John Clare)

8 The Man He Killed (Thomas Hardy)

9 Patrolling Barnegat (Walt Whitman)

10 The Little Boy Lost (William Blake)

11 Tichborne's Elegy (Charles Tichborne)

12 The Little Boy Found (William Blake)

13 The Song of the Old Mother (W. B. Yeats)

14 On my first Sonne (Ben Jonson)

15 Sonnet 130 (William Shakespeare)

16 The Laboratory (Robert Browning)

17 My Last Duchess (Robert Browning)

18 The Village Schoolmaster (Oliver Goldsmith)

19 Ulysses (Alfred Tennyson)

20 Sonnet (John Clare)

21 Inversnaid (Gerard Manley Hopkins)

22 The Eagle (Alfred Tennyson)

NOTES

Maya Angelou
I Know Why the Caged Bird Sings

Jane Austen
Pride and Prejudice

Alan Ayckbourn
Absent Friends

Elizabeth Barrett Browning
Selected Poems

Robert Bolt
A Man for All Seasons

Harold Brighouse
Hobson's Choice

Charlotte Brontë
Jane Eyre

Emily Brontë
Wuthering Heights

Shelagh Delaney
A Taste of Honey

Charles Dickens
David Copperfield
Great Expectations
Hard Times
Oliver Twist

Roddy Doyle
Paddy Clarke Ha Ha Ha

George Eliot
Silas Marner
The Mill on the Floss

Anne Frank
The Diary of a Young Girl

William Golding
Lord of the Flies

Oliver Goldsmith
She Stoops to Conquer

Willis Hall
The Long and the Short and the Tall

Thomas Hardy
Far from the Madding Crowd

The Mayor of Casterbridge
Tess of the d'Urbervilles
The Withered Arm and other Wessex Tales

L.P. Hartley
The Go-Between

Seamus Heaney
Selected Poems

Susan Hill
I'm the King of the Castle

Barry Hines
A Kestrel for a Knave

Louise Lawrence
Children of the Dust

Harper Lee
To Kill a Mockingbird

Laurie Lee
Cider with Rosie

Arthur Miller
The Crucible
A View from the Bridge

Robert O'Brien
Z for Zachariah

Frank O'Connor
My Oedipus Complex and Other Stories

George Orwell
Animal Farm

J.B. Priestley
An Inspector Calls
When We Are Married

Willy Russell
Educating Rita
Our Day Out

J.D. Salinger
The Catcher in the Rye

William Shakespeare
Henry IV Part I
Henry V
Julius Caesar

Macbeth
The Merchant of Venice
A Midsummer Night's Dream
Much Ado About Nothing
Romeo and Juliet
The Tempest
Twelfth Night

George Bernard Shaw
Pygmalion

Mary Shelley
Frankenstein

R.C. Sherriff
Journey's End

Rukshana Smith
Salt on the snow

John Steinbeck
Of Mice and Men

Robert Louis Stevenson
Dr Jekyll and Mr Hyde

Jonathan Swift
Gulliver's Travels

Robert Swindells
Daz 4 Zoe

Mildred D. Taylor
Roll of Thunder, Hear My Cry

Mark Twain
Huckleberry Finn

James Watson
Talking in Whispers

Edith Wharton
Ethan Frome

William Wordsworth
Selected Poems

A Choice of Poets

Mystery Stories of the Nineteenth Century including The Signalman

Nineteenth Century Short Stories

Poetry of the First World War

Six Women Poets

Margaret Atwood
Cat's Eye
The Handmaid's Tale

Jane Austen
Emma
Mansfield Park
Persuasion
Pride and Prejudice
Sense and Sensibility

Alan Bennett
Talking Heads

William Blake
Songs of Innocence and of Experience

Charlotte Brontë
Jane Eyre
Villette

Emily Brontë
Wuthering Heights

Angela Carter
Nights at the Circus

Geoffrey Chaucer
The Franklin's Prologue and Tale
The Miller's Prologue and Tale
The Prologue to the Canterbury Tales
The Wife of Bath's Prologue and Tale

Samuel Coleridge
Selected Poems

Joseph Conrad
Heart of Darkness

Daniel Defoe
Moll Flanders

Charles Dickens
Bleak House
Great Expectations
Hard Times

Emily Dickinson
Selected Poems

John Donne
Selected Poems

Carol Ann Duffy
Selected Poems

George Eliot
Middlemarch
The Mill on the Floss

T.S. Eliot
Selected Poems
The Waste Land

F. Scott Fitzgerald
The Great Gatsby

E.M. Forster
A Passage to India

Brian Friel
Translations

Thomas Hardy
Jude the Obscure
The Mayor of Casterbridge
The Return of the Native
Selected Poems
Tess of the d'Urbervilles

Seamus Heaney
Selected Poems from 'Opened Ground'

Nathaniel Hawthorne
The Scarlet Letter

Homer
The Illad
The Odyssey

Aldous Huxley
Brave New World

Kazuo Ishiguro
The Remains of the Day

Ben Jonson
The Alchemist

James Joyce
Dubliners

John Keats
Selected Poems

Christopher Marlowe
Doctor Faustus
Edward II

Arthur Miller
Death of a Salesman

John Milton
Paradise Lost Books I & II

Toni Morrison
Beloved

George Orwell
Nineteen Eighty-Four

Sylvia Plath
Selected Poems

Alexander Pope
Rape of the Lock & Selected Poems

William Shakespeare
Antony and Cleopatra
As You Like It
Hamlet
Henry IV Part I
King Lear
Macbeth
Measure for Measure
The Merchant of Venice
A Midsummer Night's Dream
Much Ado About Nothing
Othello
Richard II
Richard III
Romeo and Juliet
The Taming of the Shrew
The Tempest
Twelfth Night
The Winter's Tale

George Bernard Shaw
Saint Joan

Mary Shelley
Frankenstein

Jonathan Swift
Gulliver's Travels and A Modest Proposal

Alfred Tennyson
Selected Poems

Virgil
The Aeneid

Alice Walker
The Color Purple

Oscar Wilde
The Importance of Being Earnest

Tennessee Williams
A Streetcar Named Desire

Jeanette Winterson
Oranges Are Not the Only Fruit

John Webster
The Duchess of Malfi

Virginia Woolf
To the Lighthouse

W.B. Yeats
Selected Poems

Metaphysical Poets